they can talk

they can talk

a collection of comics about animals

by jimmy craig

Ulysses Press

Ulysses Press
P.O. Box 3440
Berkeley, CA 94703
www.ulyssespress.com

ISBN 978-1-61243-783-5
Library of Congress Catalog Number: 2017959364

Printed in Korea by WE SP through Four Colour Print Group
10 9 8 7 6 5 4 3 2 1

Acquisitions Editor: Casie Vogel
Managing Editor: Claire Chun
Proofreader: Renee Rutledge

Distributed by Publishers Group West

for Jenna

introduction

They can talk, we just can't understand them.

My name's Jimmy. I don't have a degree in linguistics or animal sciences, but I've taken it upon myself to assume the role of the Unofficial Interpreter of the Animal Kingdom. I've always liked animals—I even like dogs *and* cats. I think that makes me more than qualified.

The following is a collection of comics illustrating what I think animals might actually be saying to us and each other.

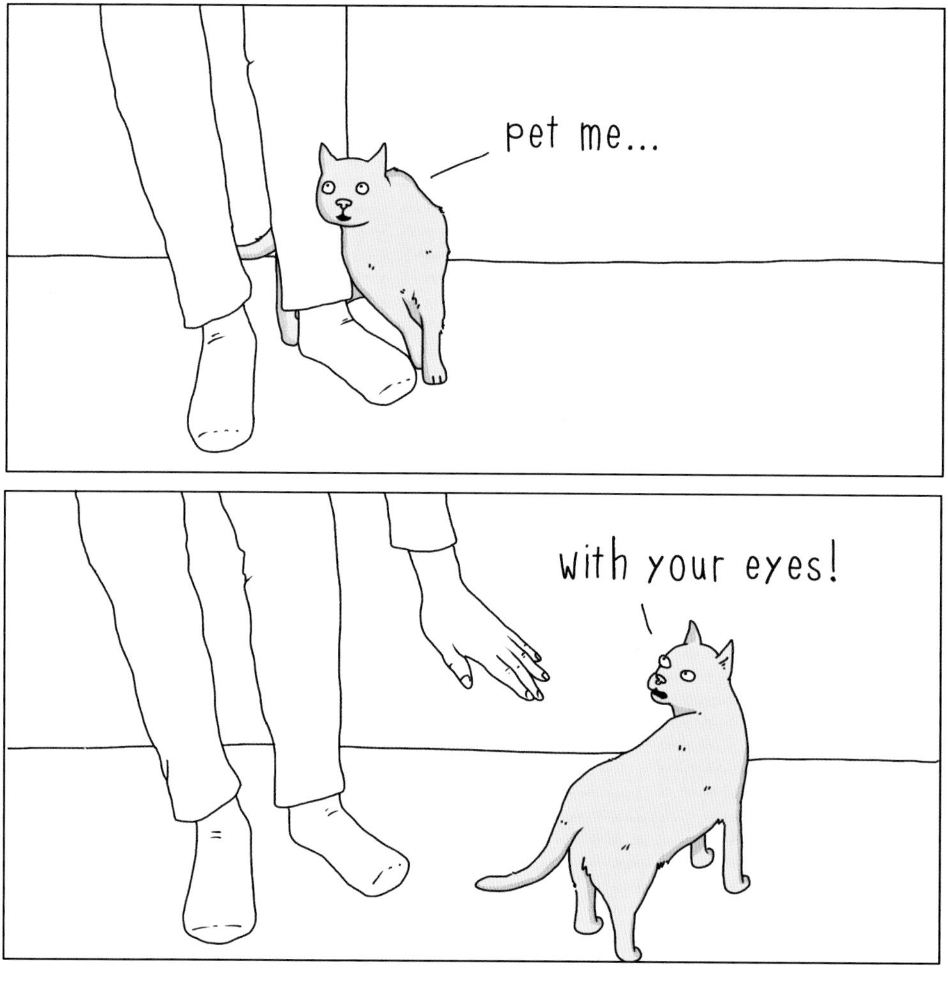
pet me...
with your eyes!

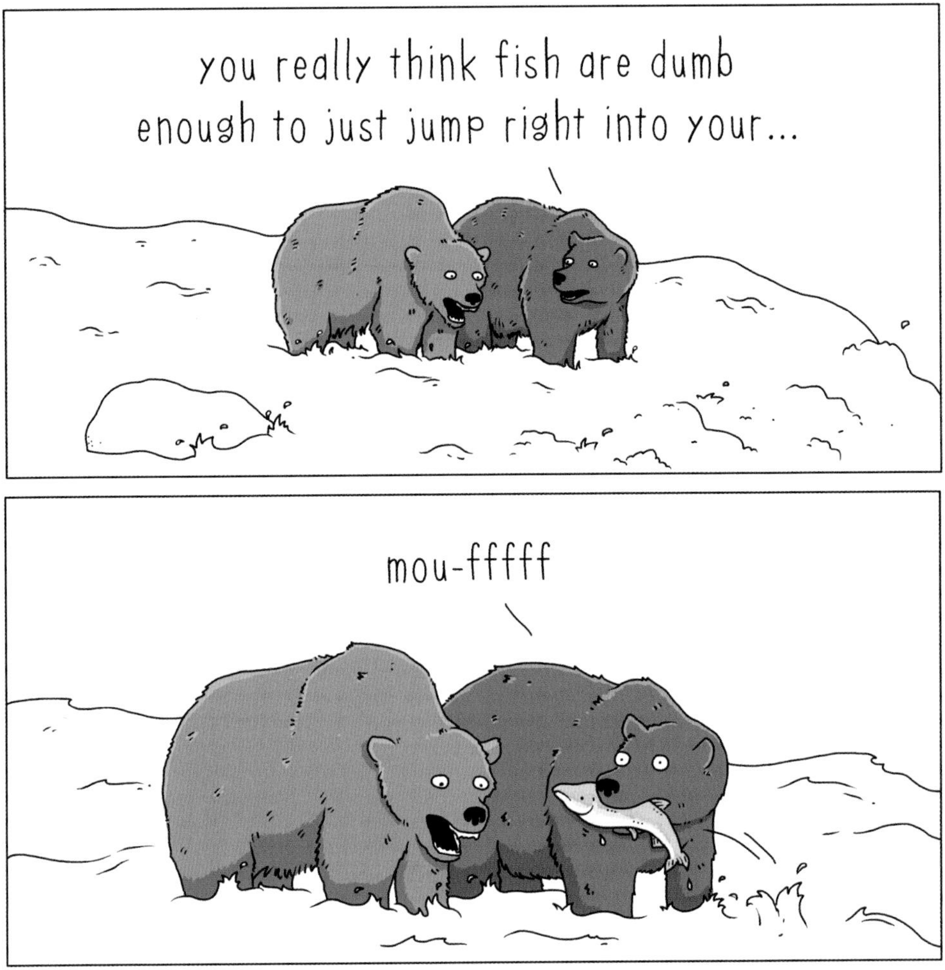
you really think fish are dumb enough to just jump right into your...
mou-fffff

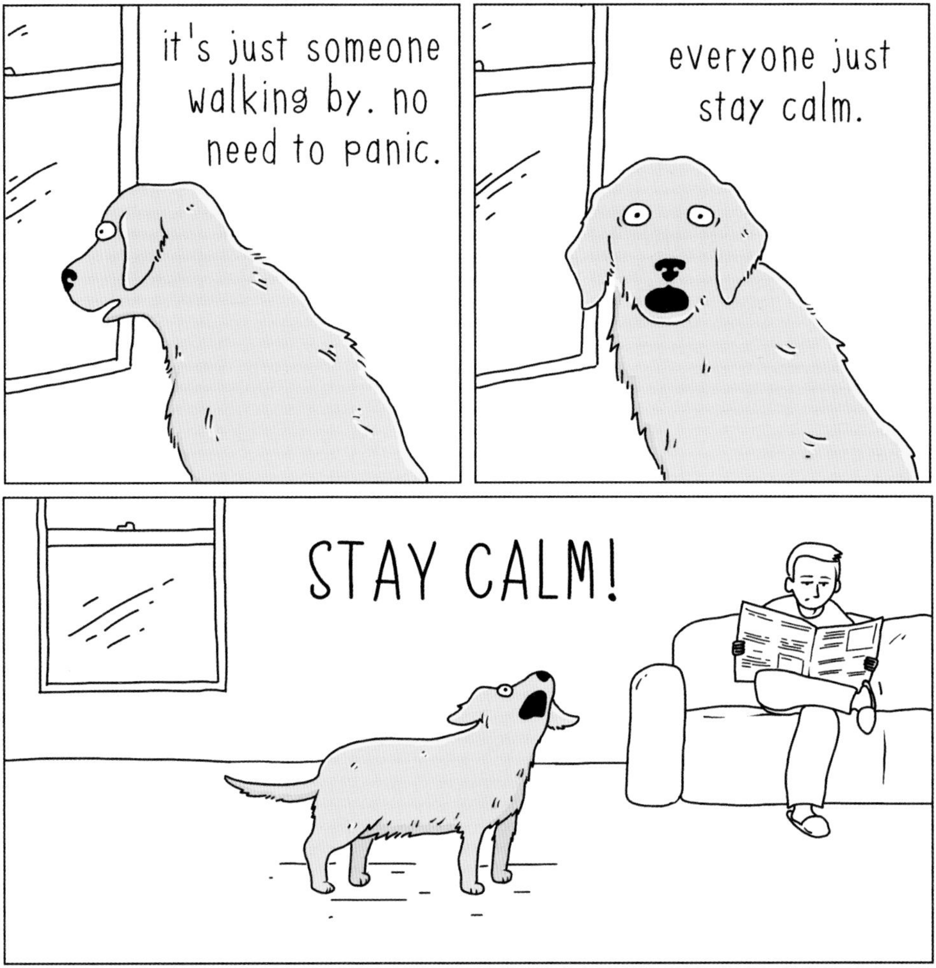
it's just someone walking by. no need to panic.
everyone just stay calm.
STAY CALM!

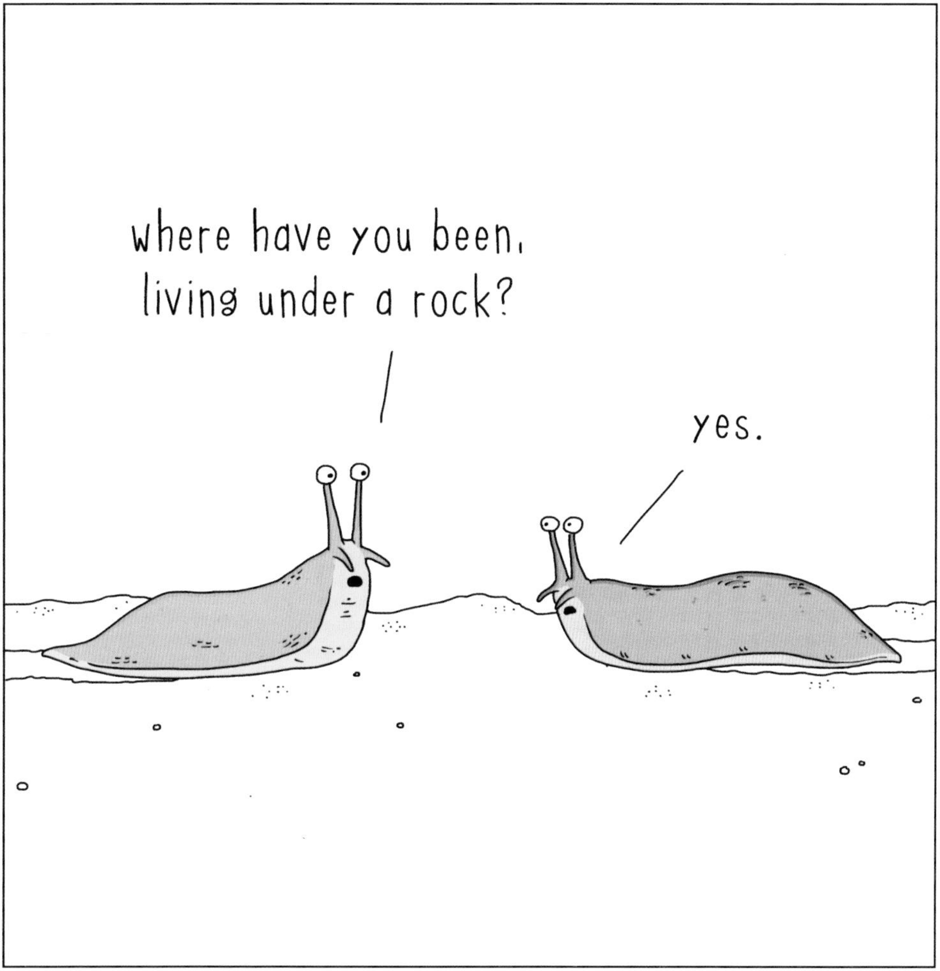
where have you been,
living under a rock?
yes.

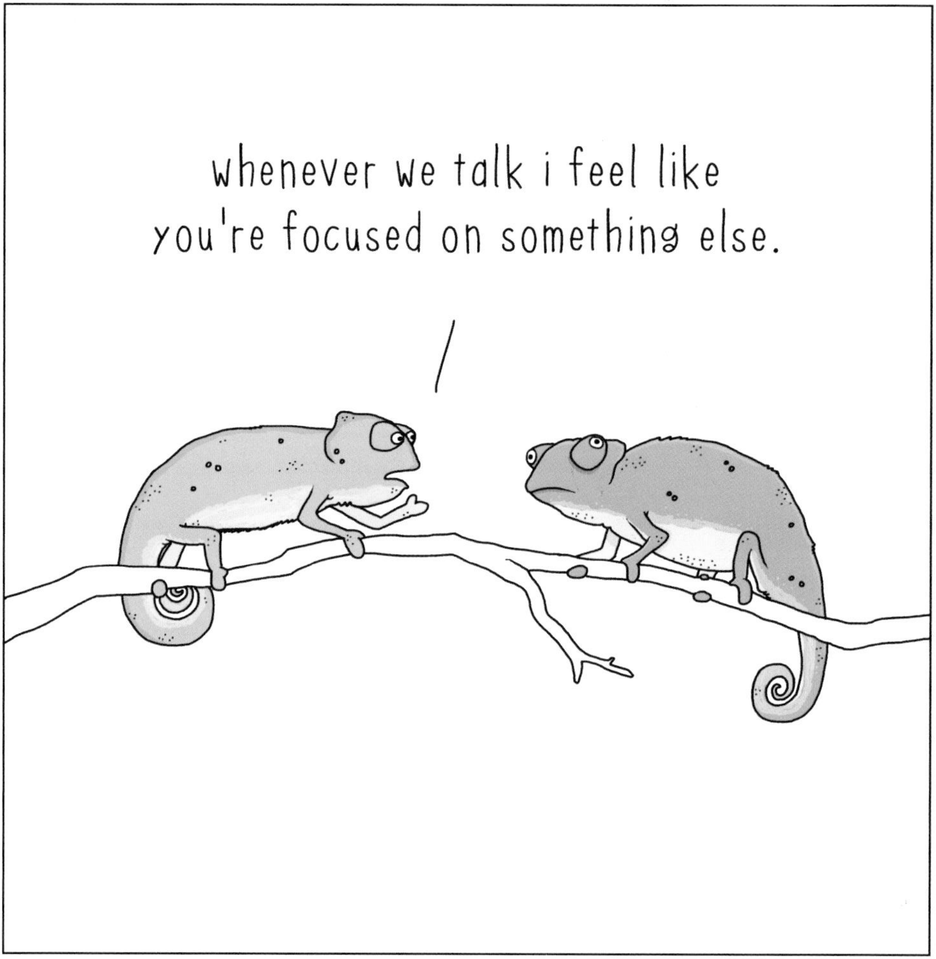
whenever we talk i feel like you're focused on something else.

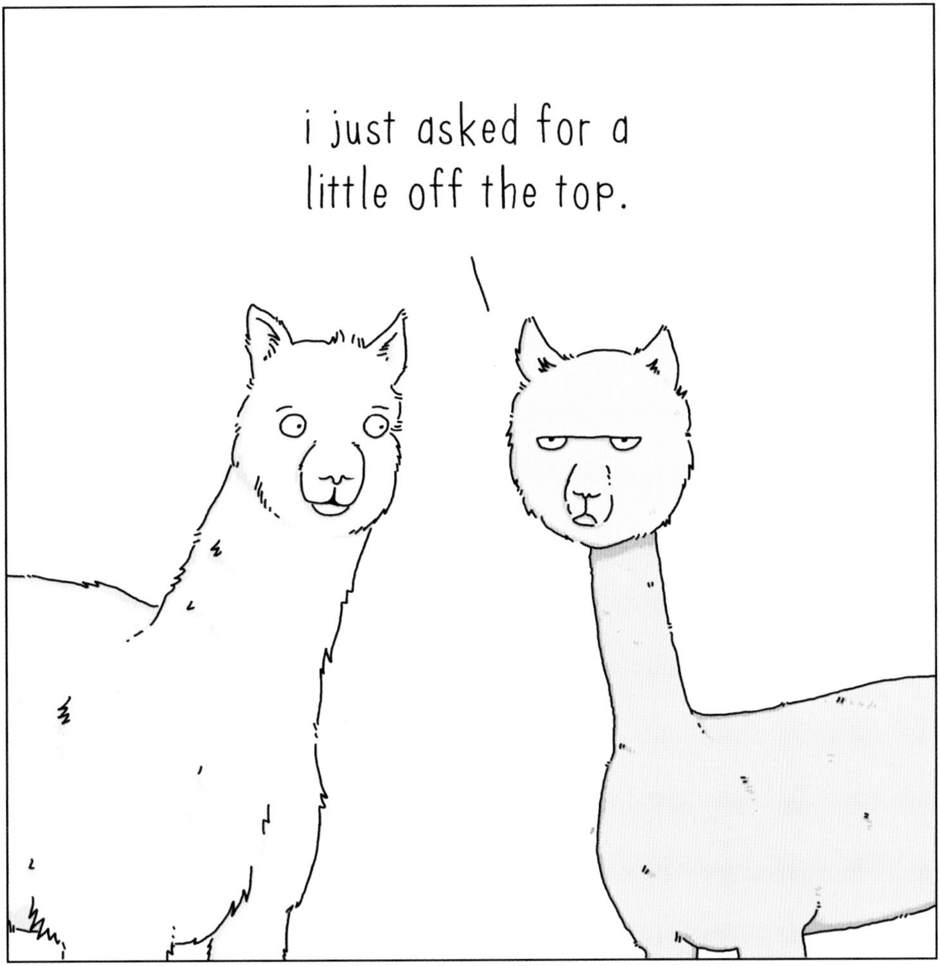
i just asked for a little off the top.

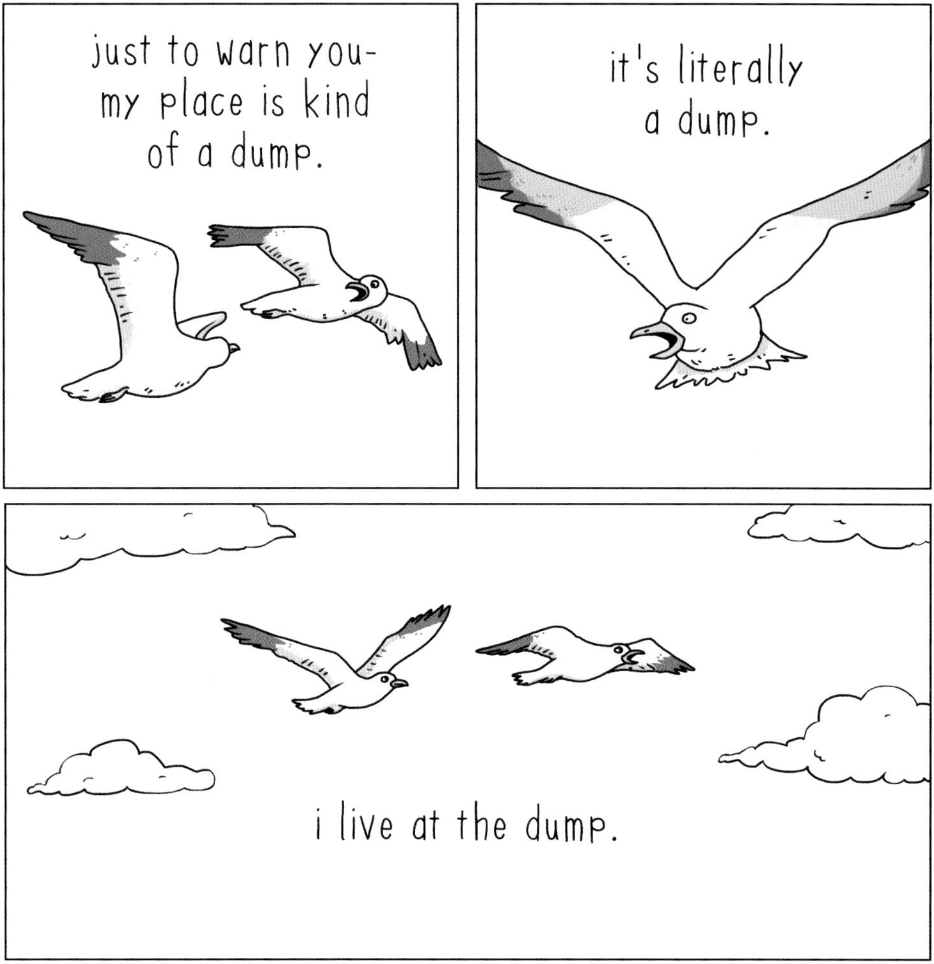
just to warn you-
my place is kind
of a dump.
it's literally
a dump.
i live at the dump.

does this rat make me look fat?

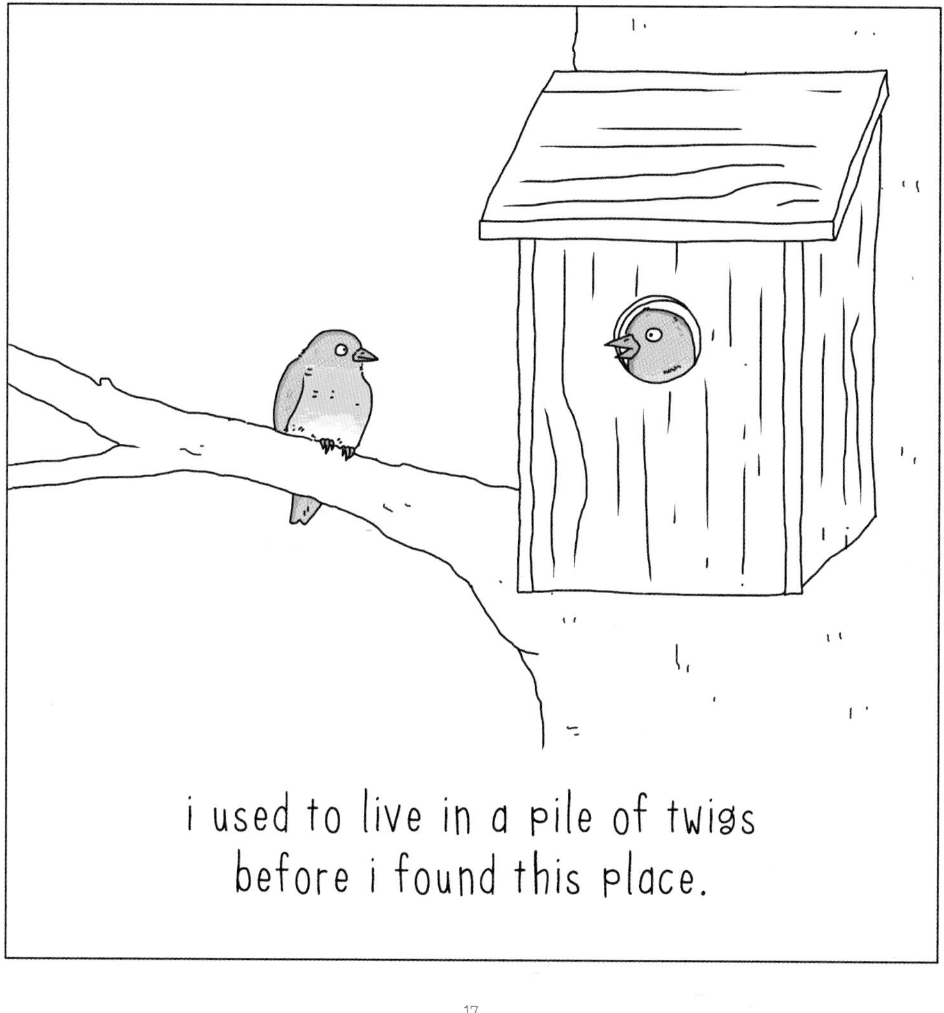

i used to live in a pile of twigs
before i found this place.

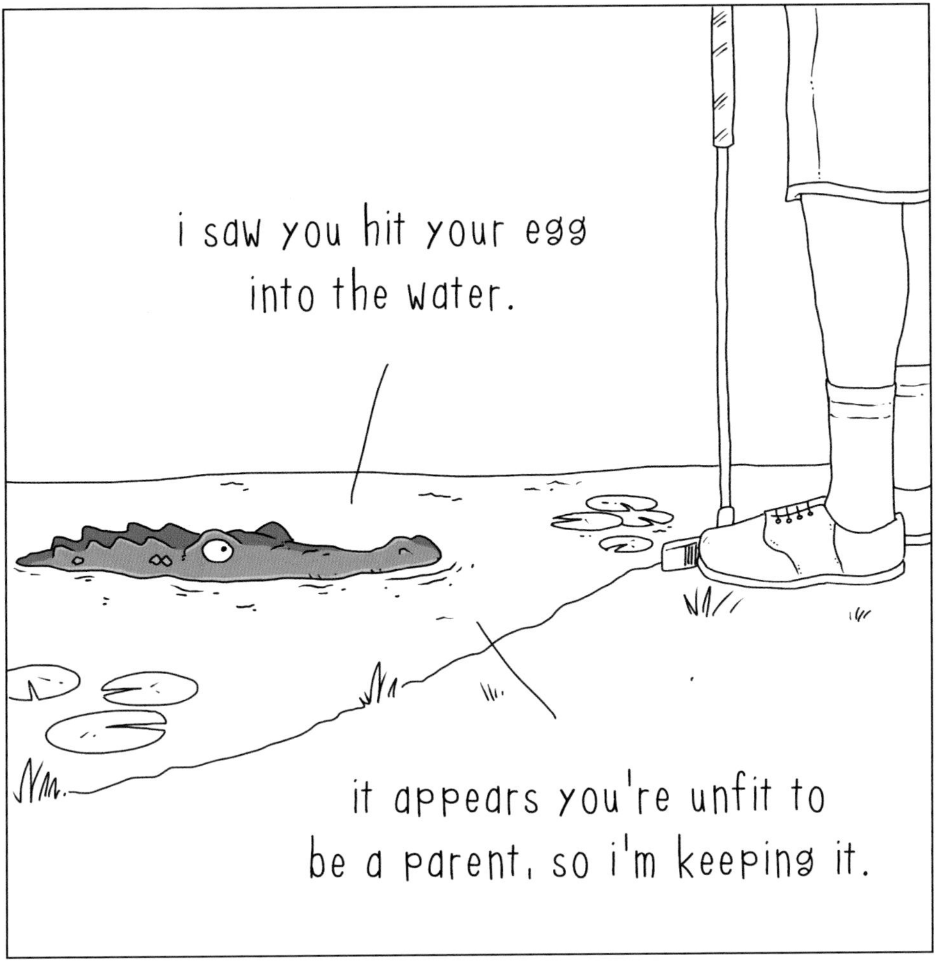
i saw you hit your egg into the water.
it appears you're unfit to be a parent, so i'm keeping it.

i have super strength!
i have super hearing!
i look like a stick!

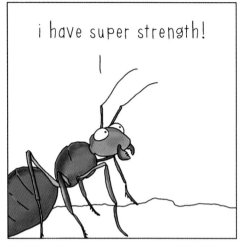

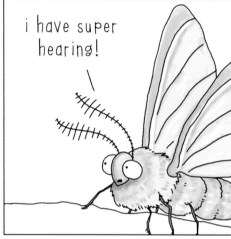

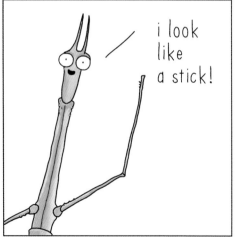

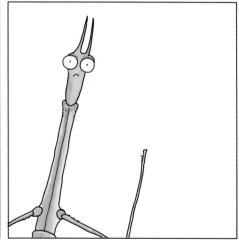

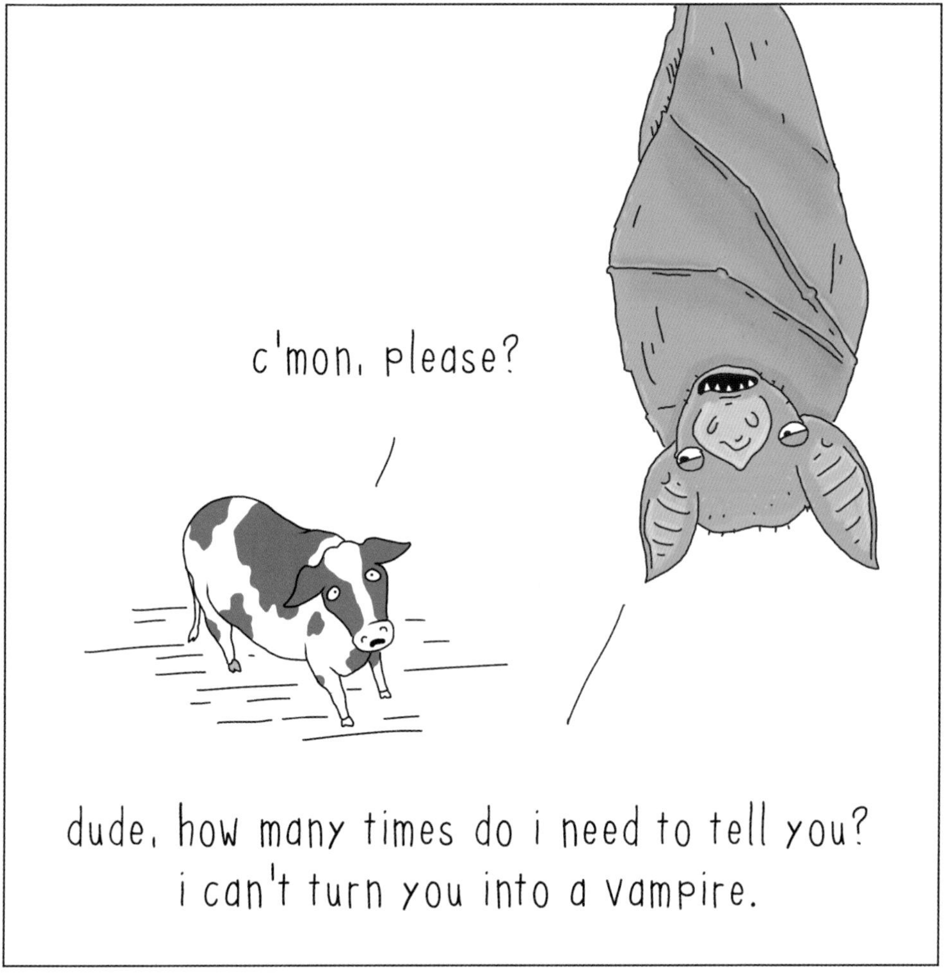
c'mon, please?
dude, how many times do i need to tell you? i can't turn you into a vampire.

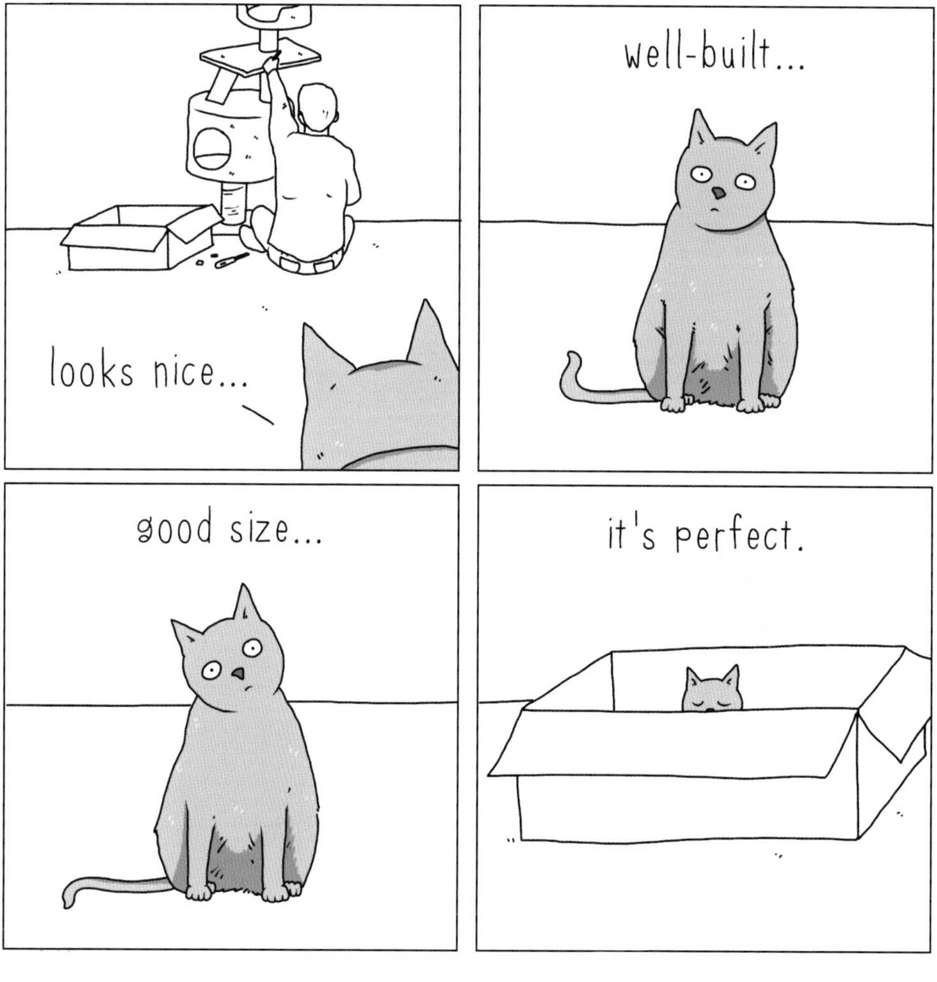
looks nice...
well-built...
good size...
it's perfect.

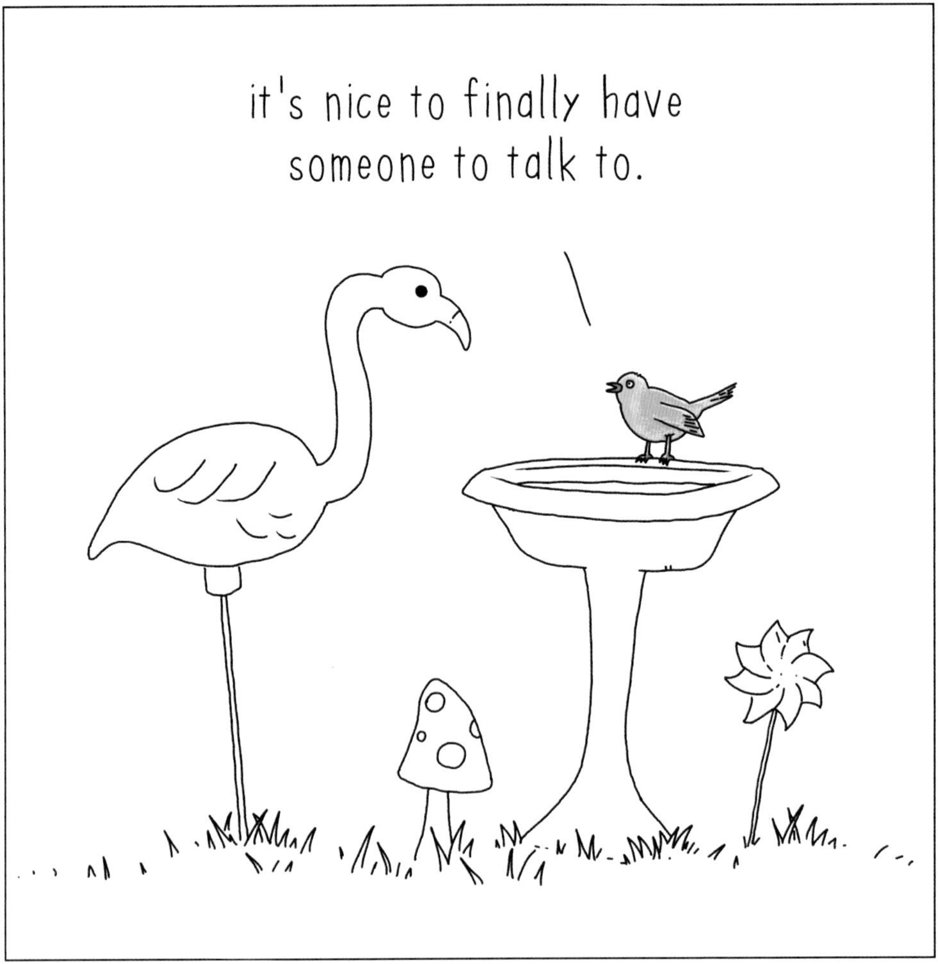
it's nice to finally have someone to talk to.

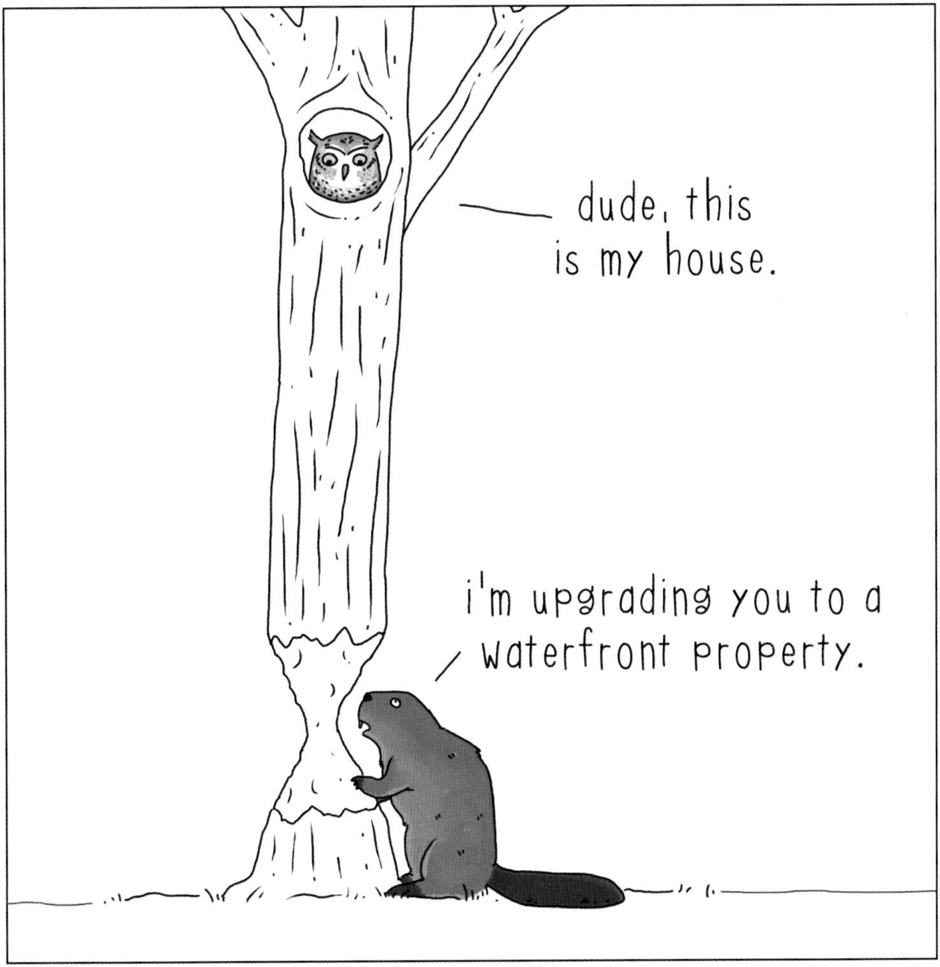
dude, this is my house.
i'm upgrading you to a waterfront property.

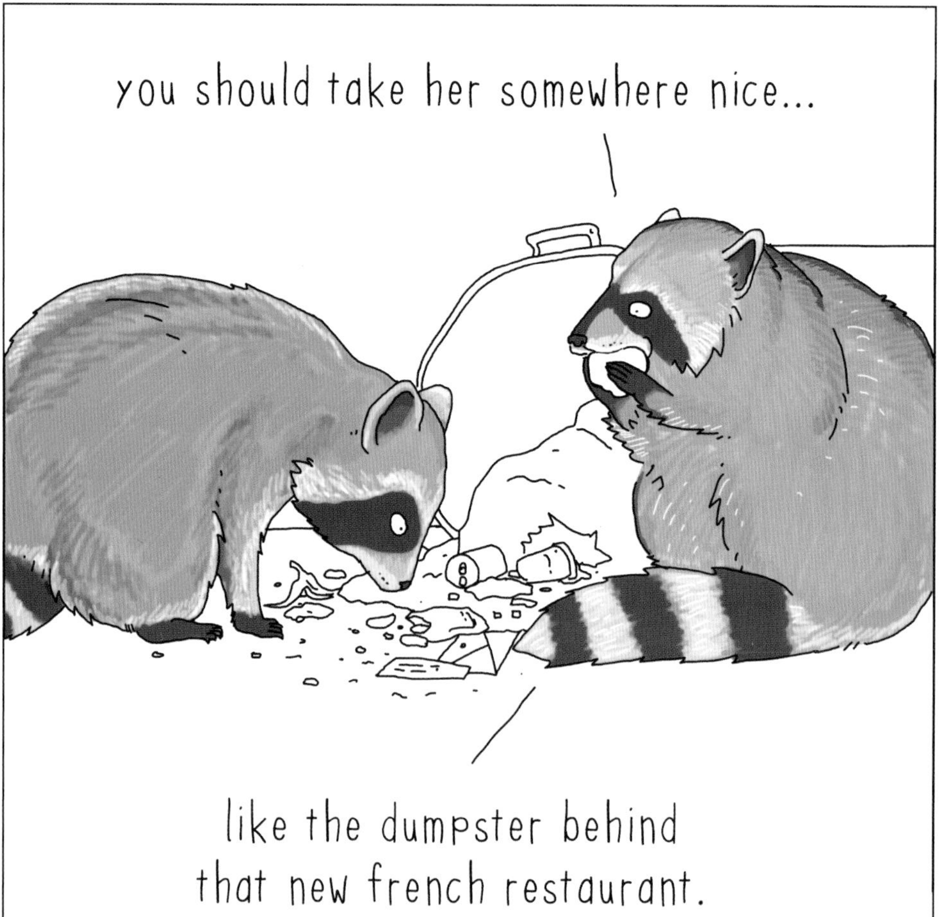
you should take her somewhere nice...
like the dumpster behind
that new french restaurant.

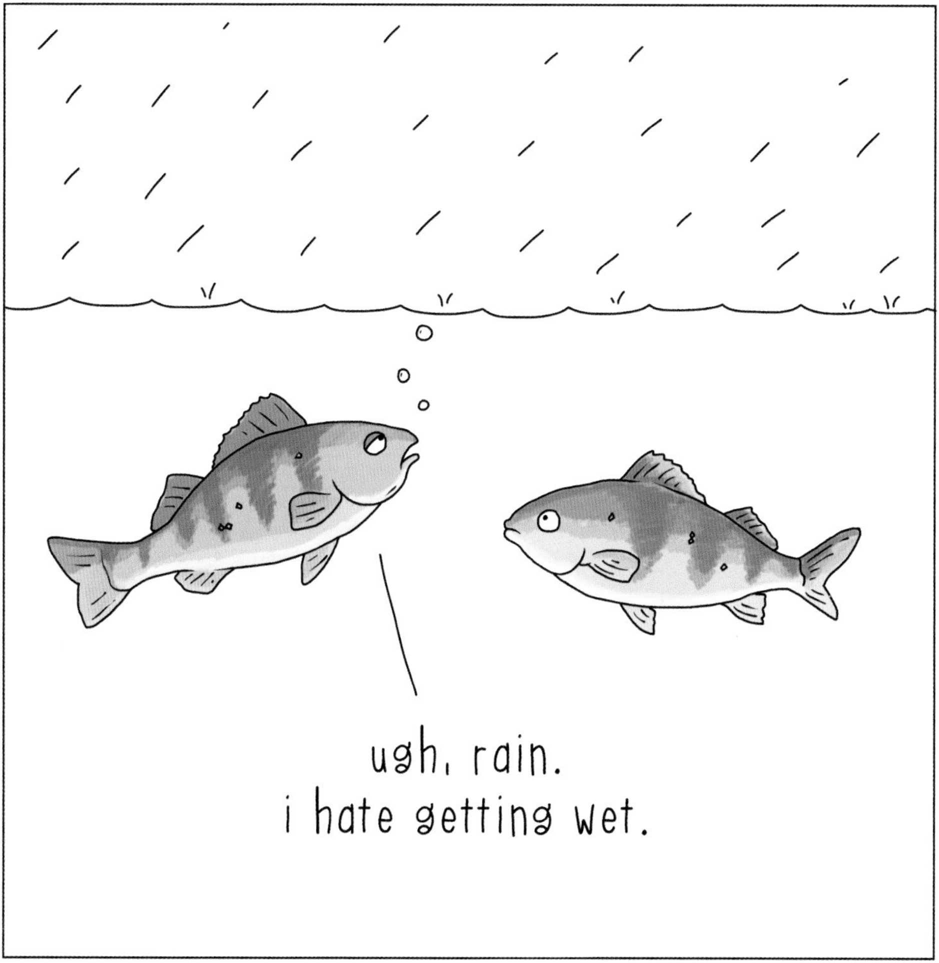
ugh, rain.
i hate getting wet.

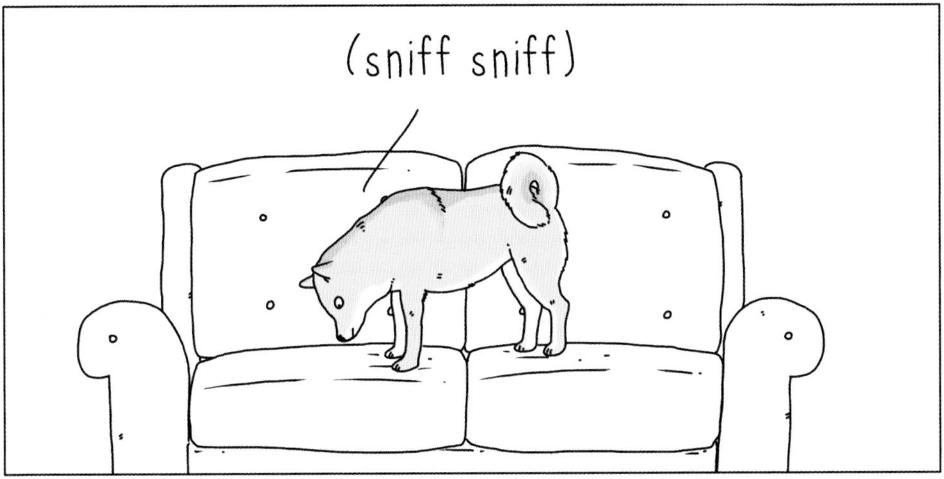
(sniff sniff)

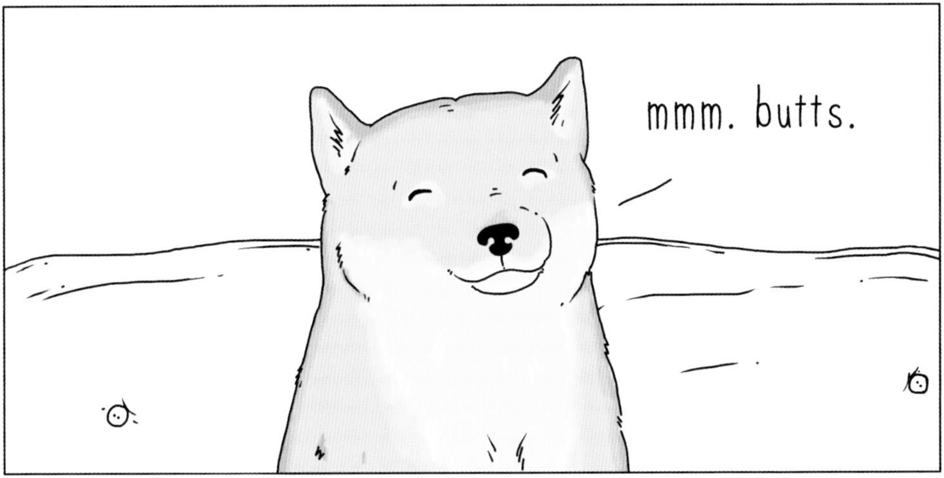
mmm. butts.

ok, now apologize and shake noses.

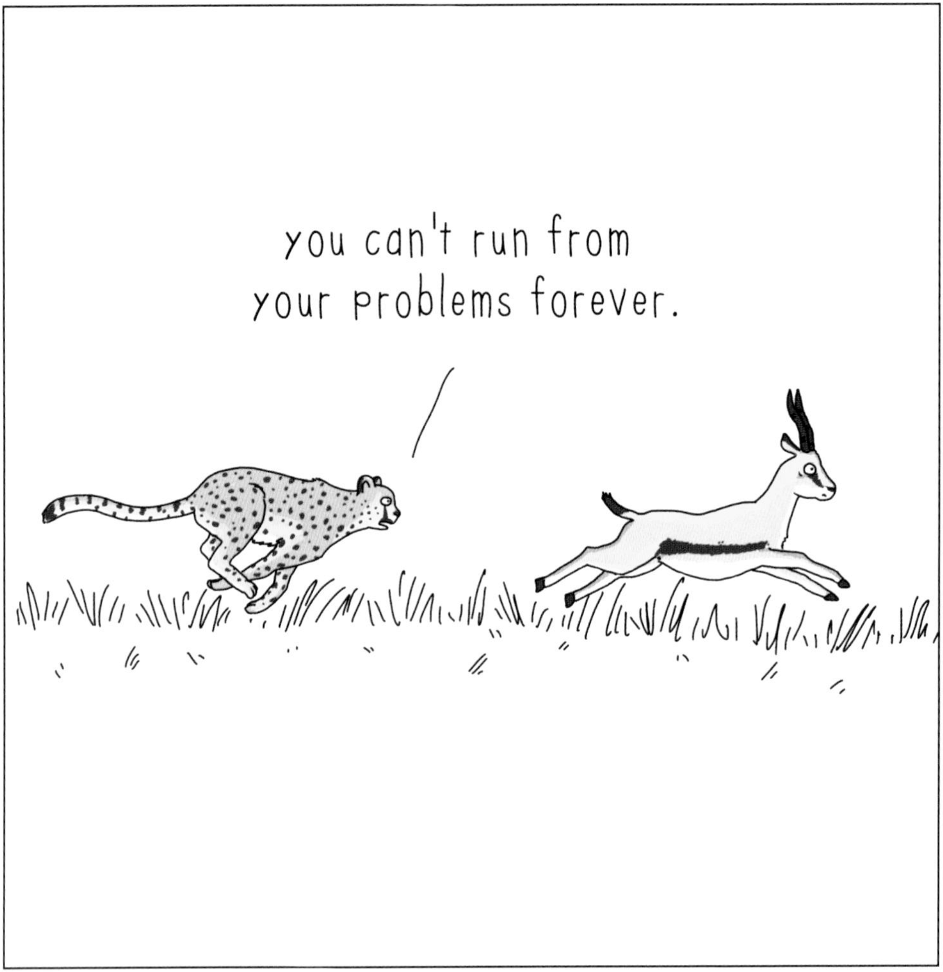
you can't run from your problems forever.

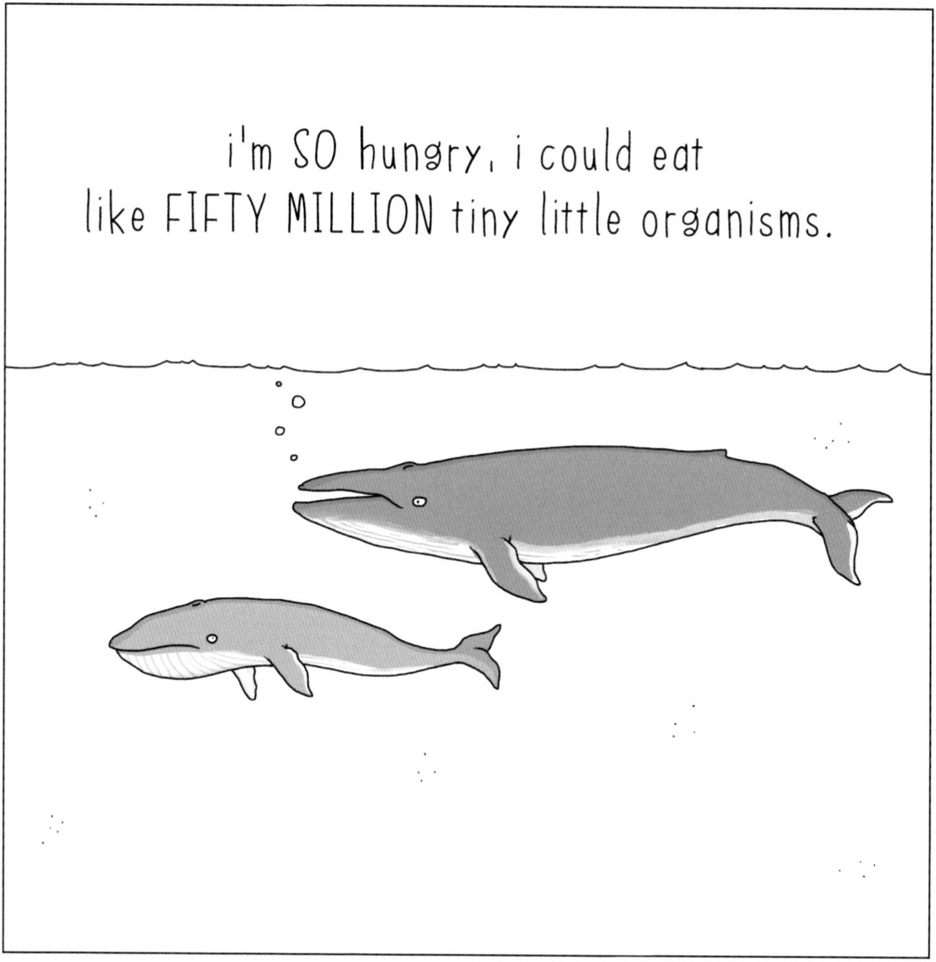
i'm SO hungry, i could eat
like FIFTY MILLION tiny little organisms.

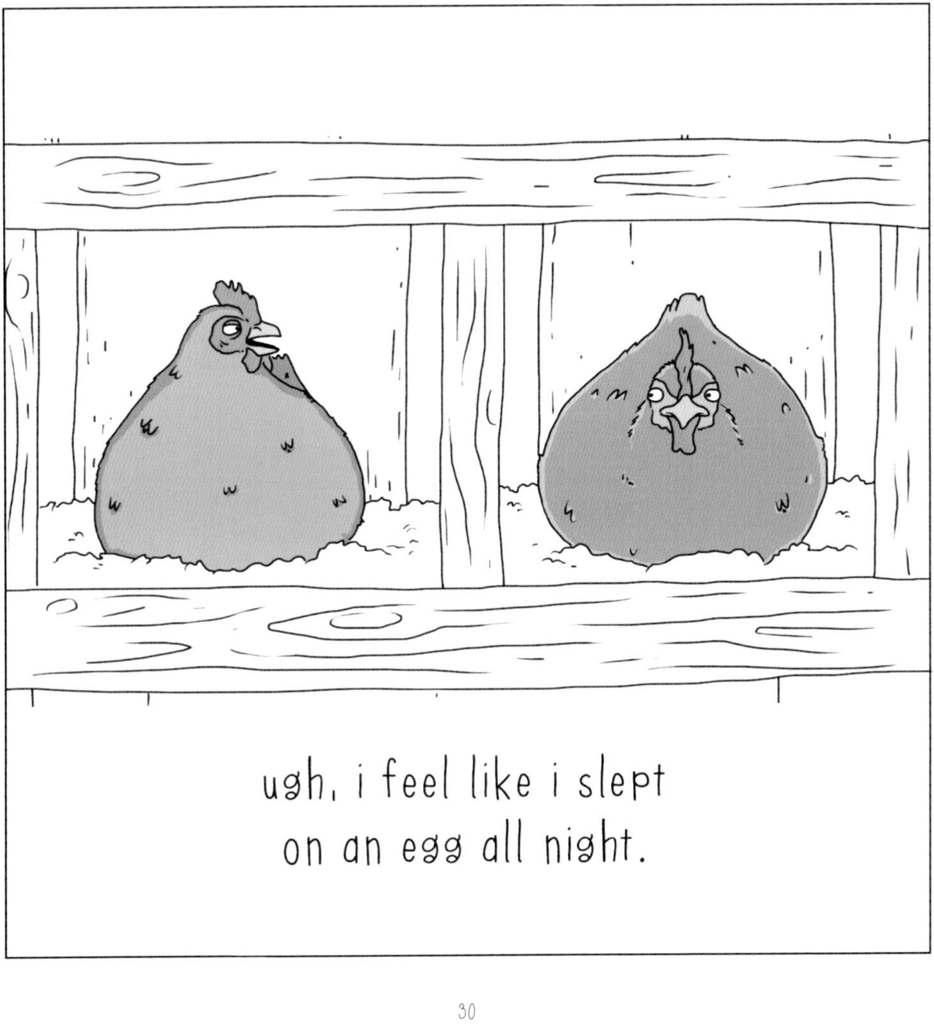

ugh, i feel like i slept
on an egg all night.

i'm more of a parking-lot gull.

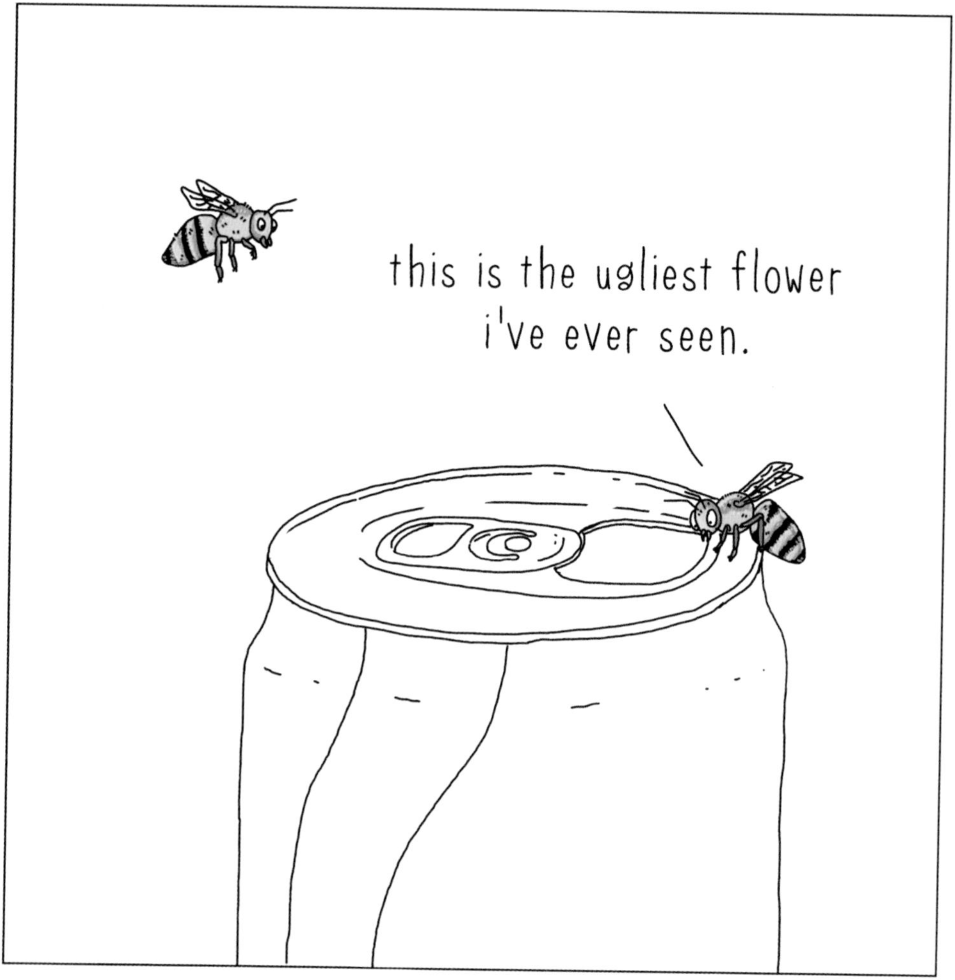
this is the ugliest flower
i've ever seen.

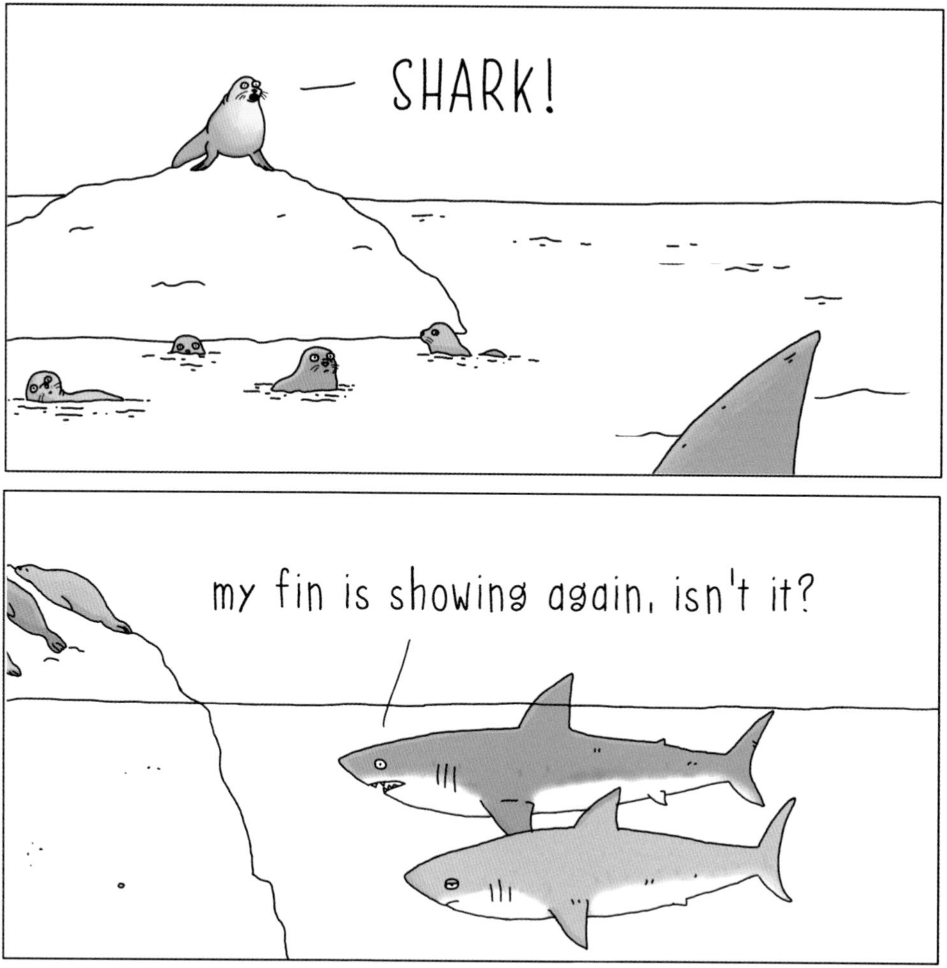
SHARK!
my fin is showing again, isn't it?

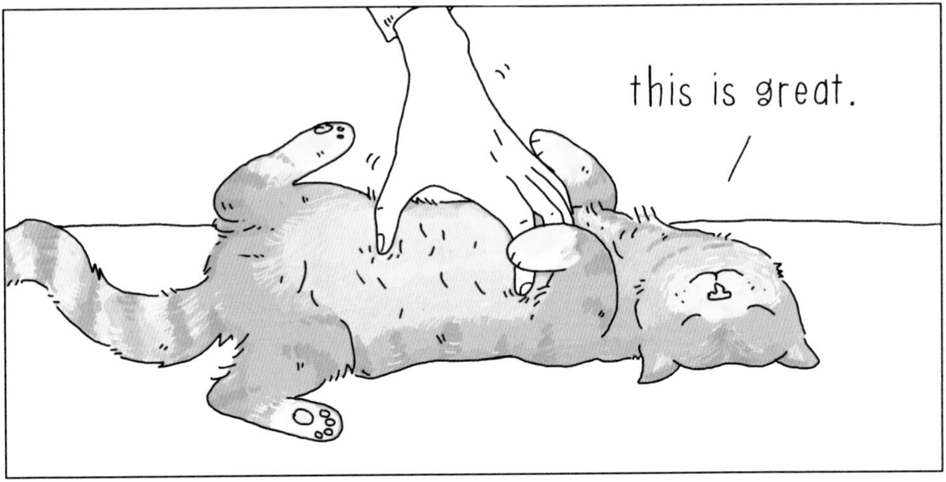
this is great.

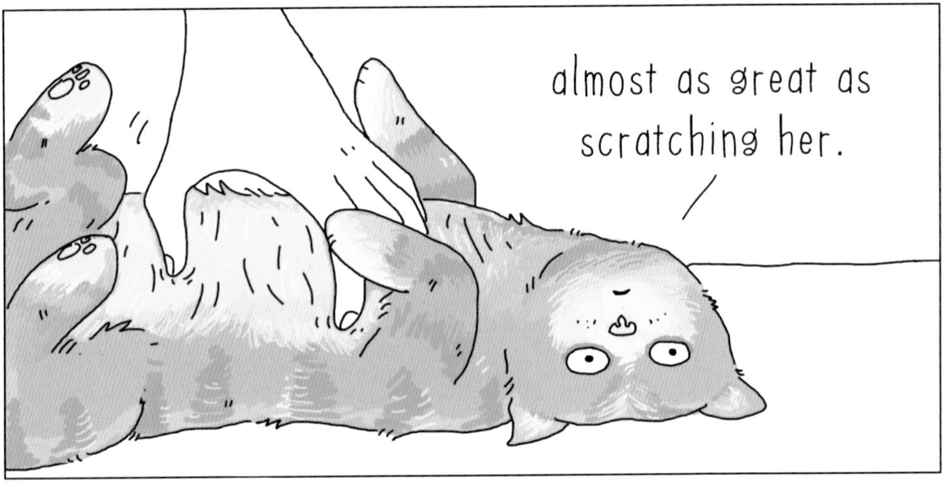
almost as great as scratching her.

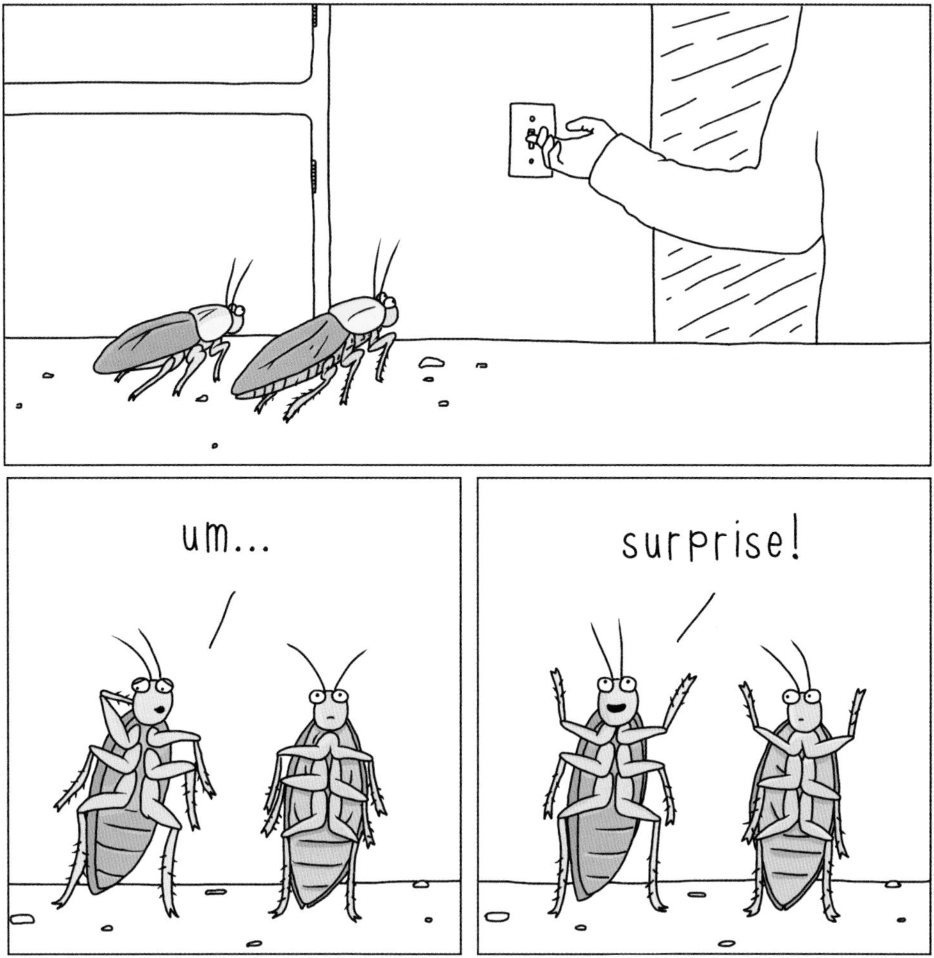
um...
surprise!

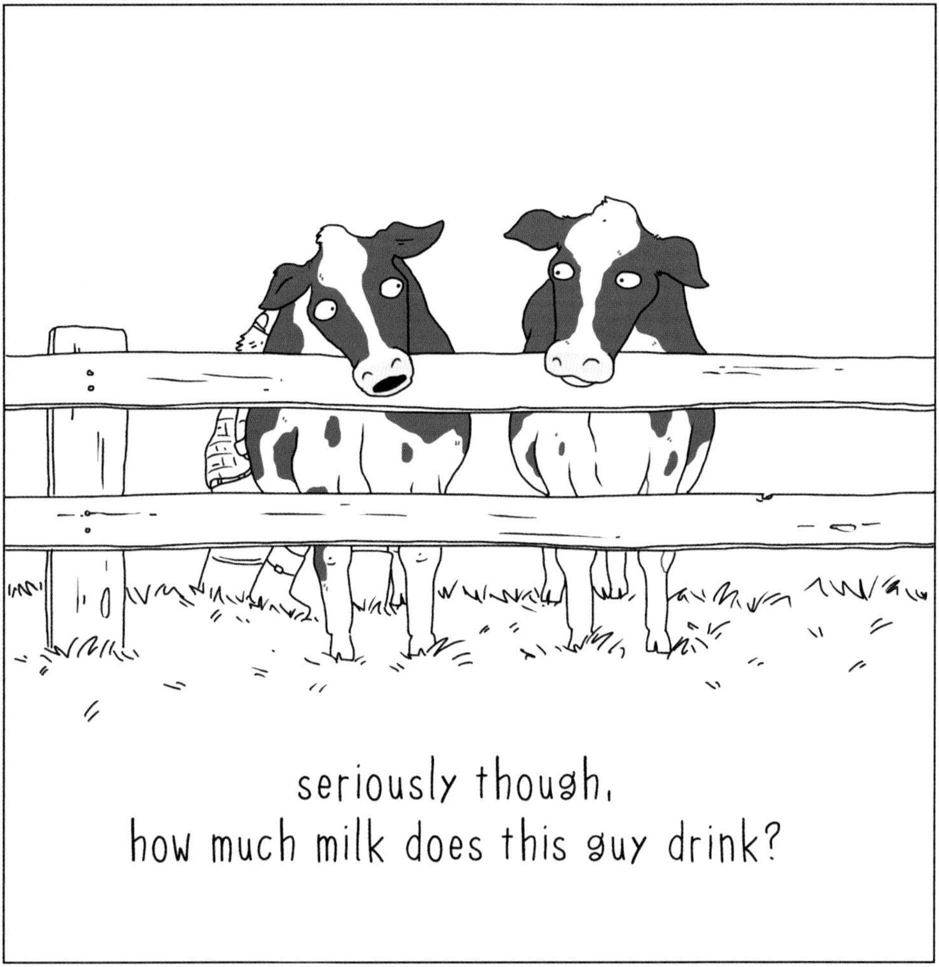
seriously though,
how much milk does this guy drink?

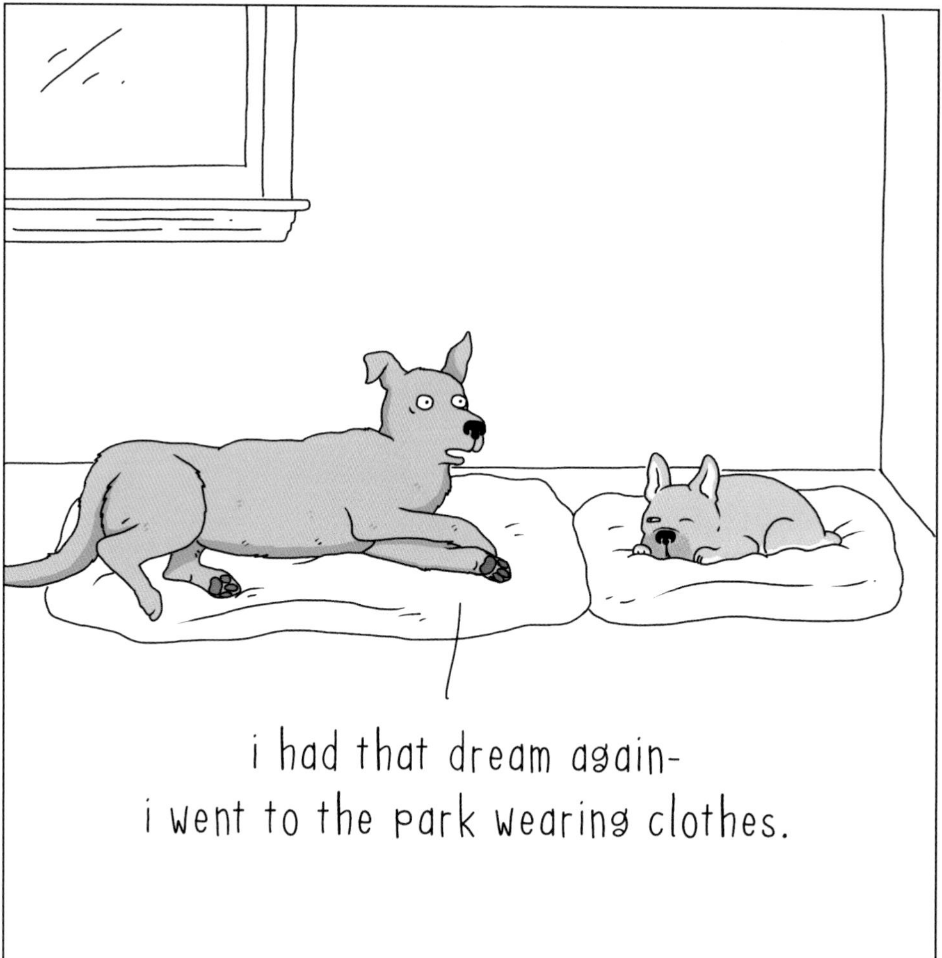
i had that dream again-
i went to the park wearing clothes.

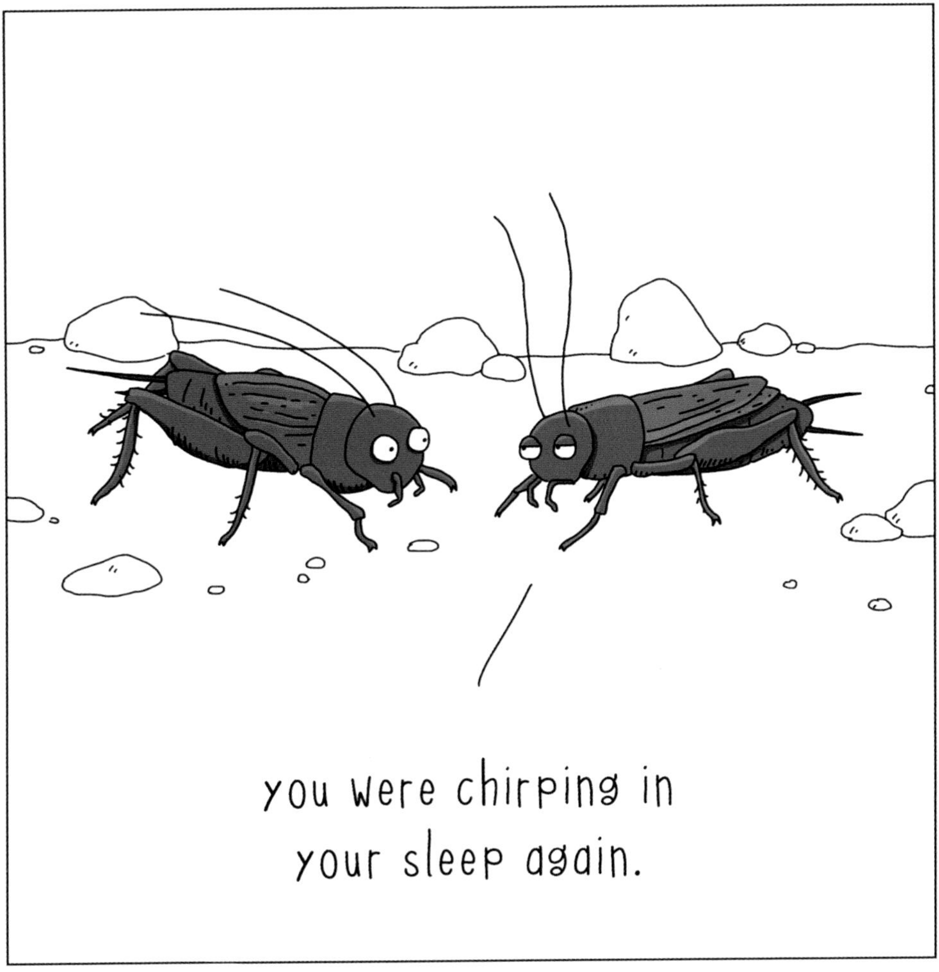
you were chirping in
your sleep again.

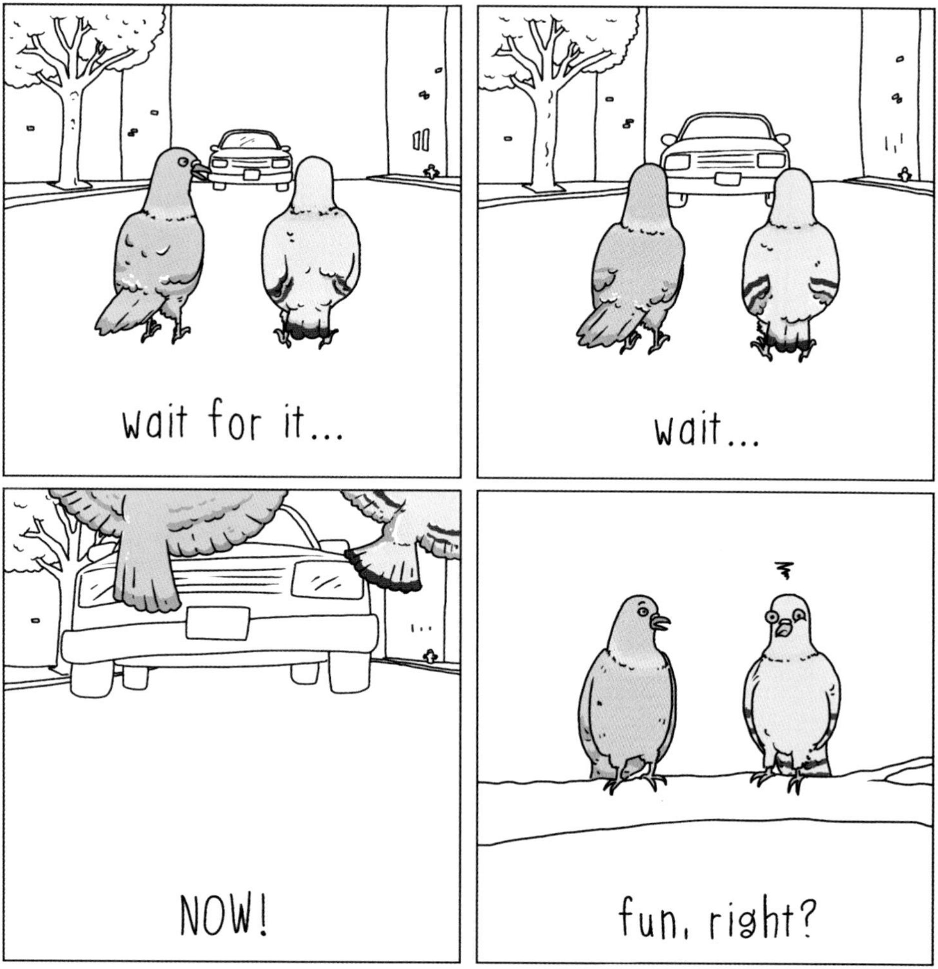
wait for it...
wait...
NOW!
fun, right?

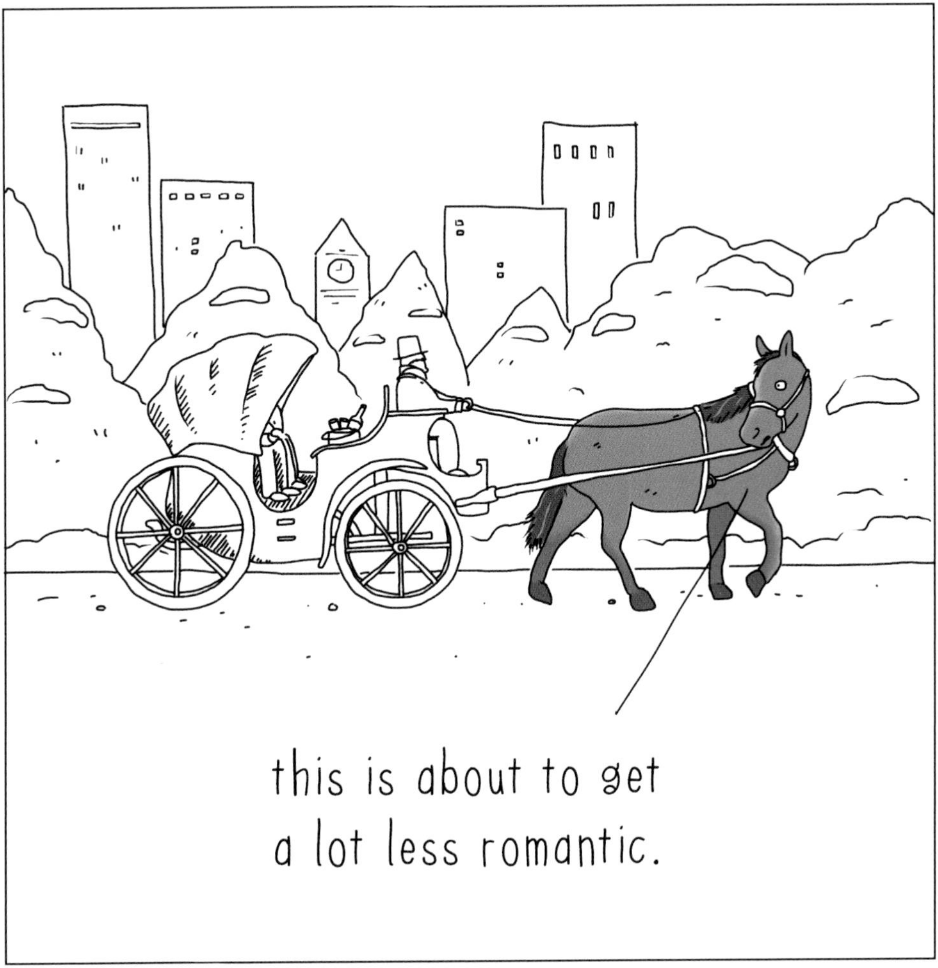
this is about to get
a lot less romantic.

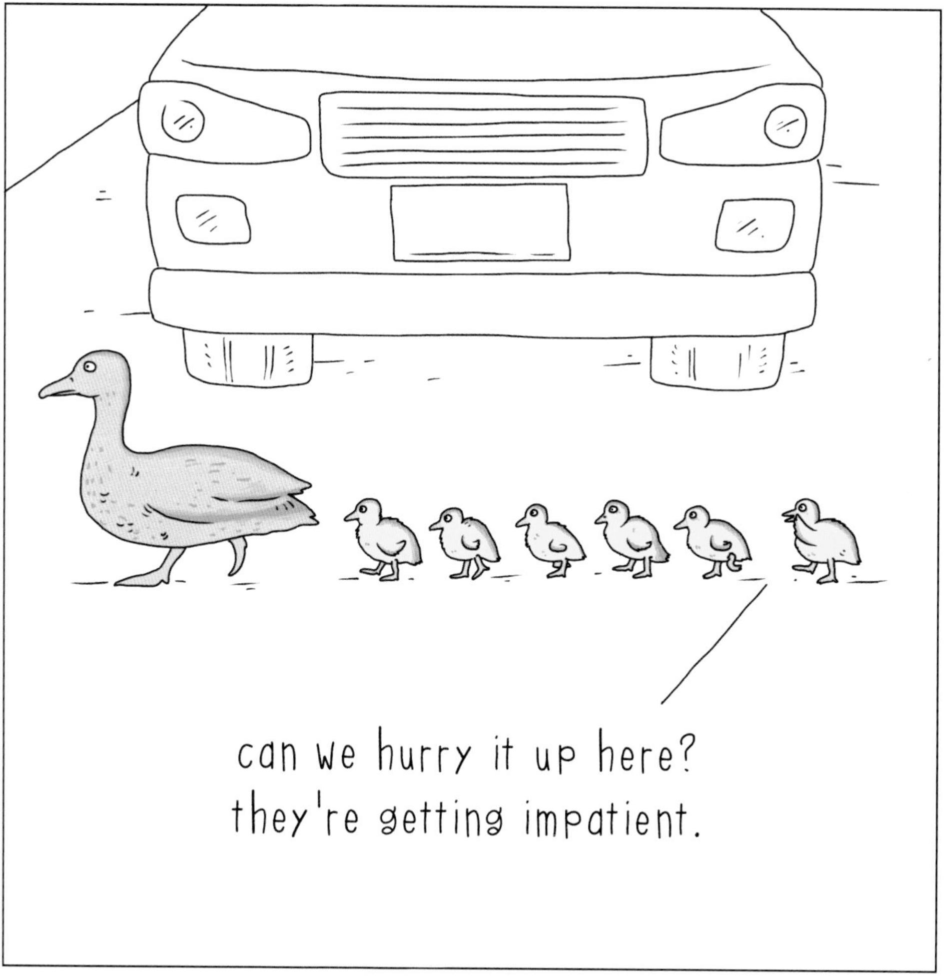
can we hurry it up here?
they're getting impatient.

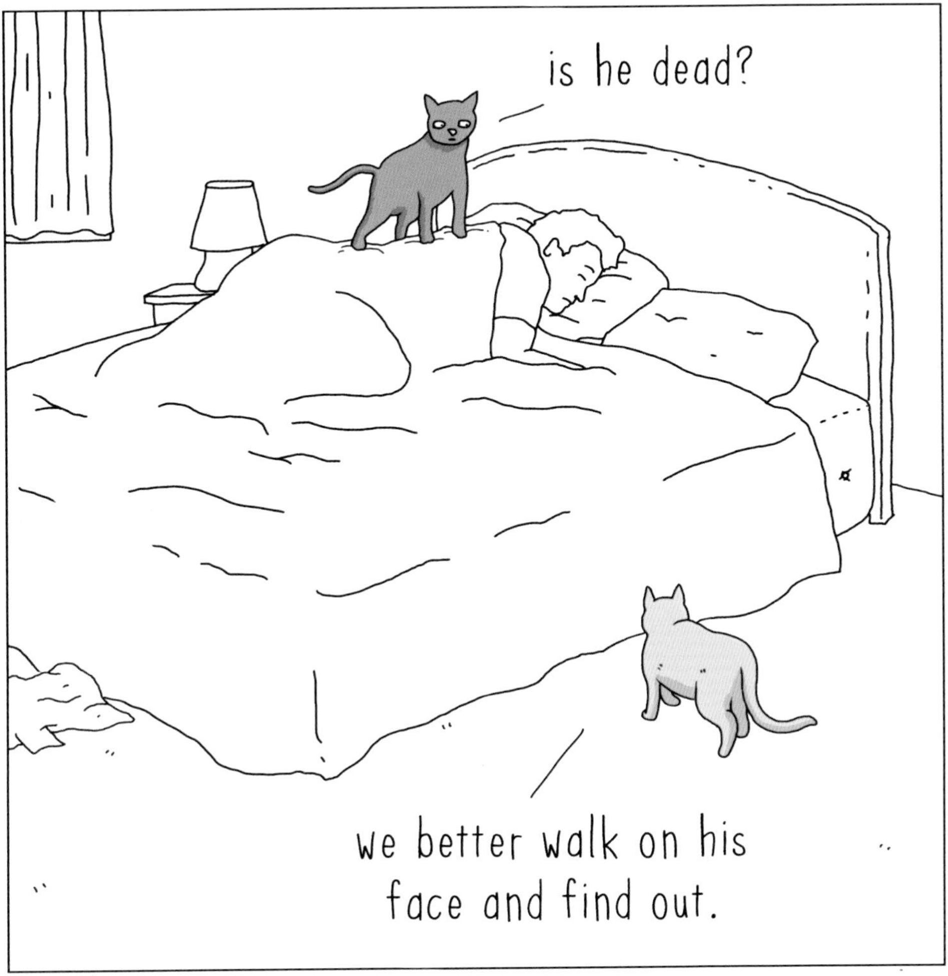
is he dead?
we better walk on his face and find out.

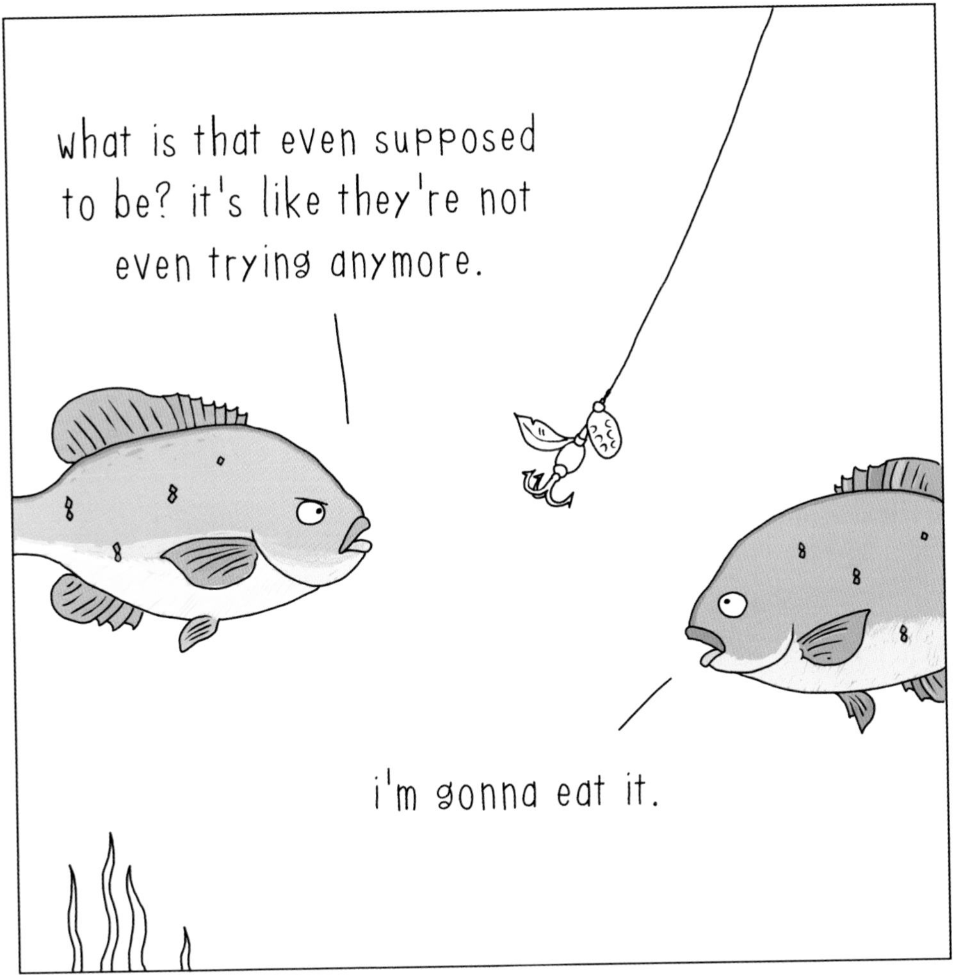
what is that even supposed to be? it's like they're not even trying anymore.
i'm gonna eat it.

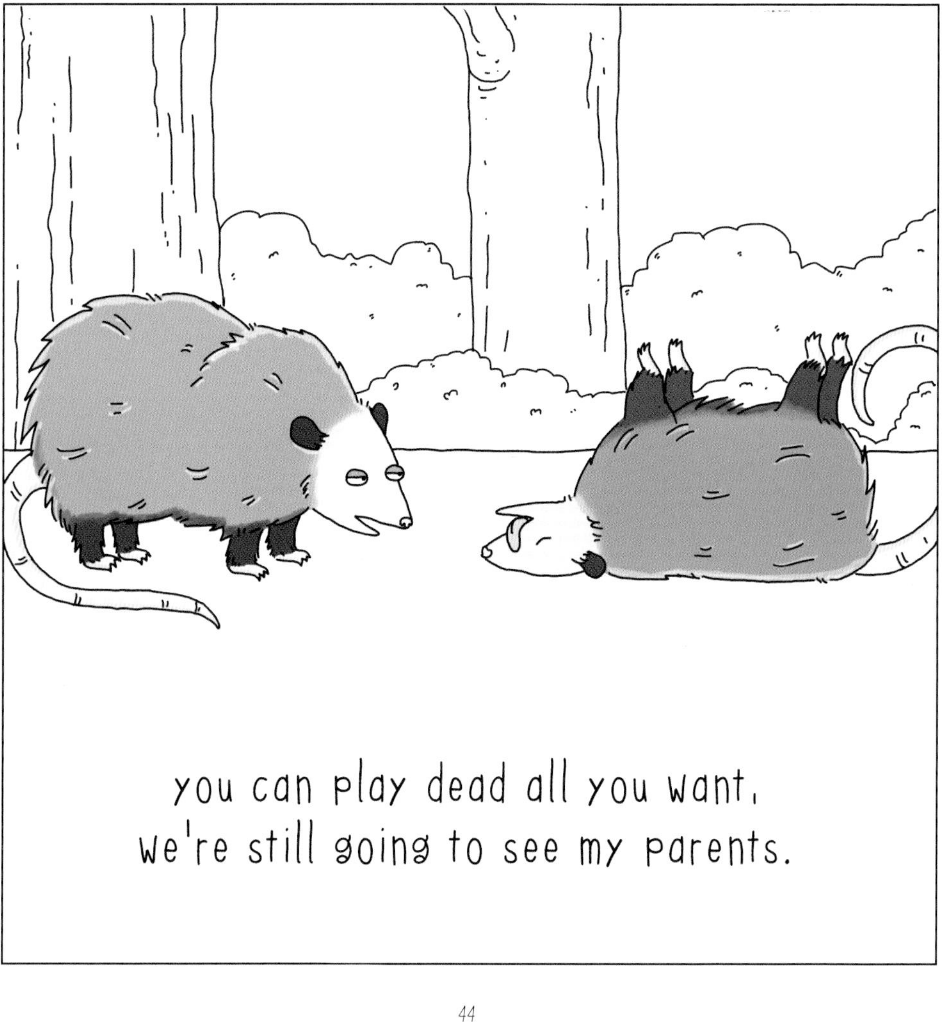

you can play dead all you want,
we're still going to see my parents.

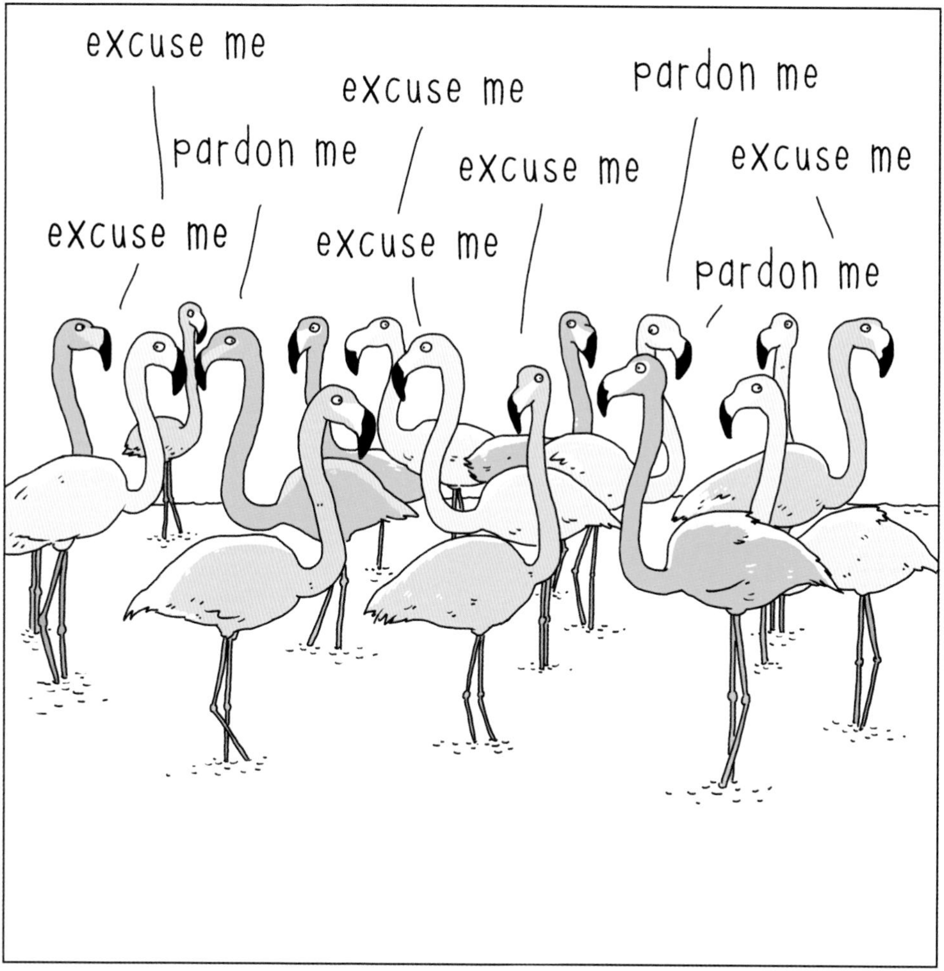
excuse me
pardon me
excuse me
excuse me
excuse me
excuse me
pardon me
excuse me
pardon me

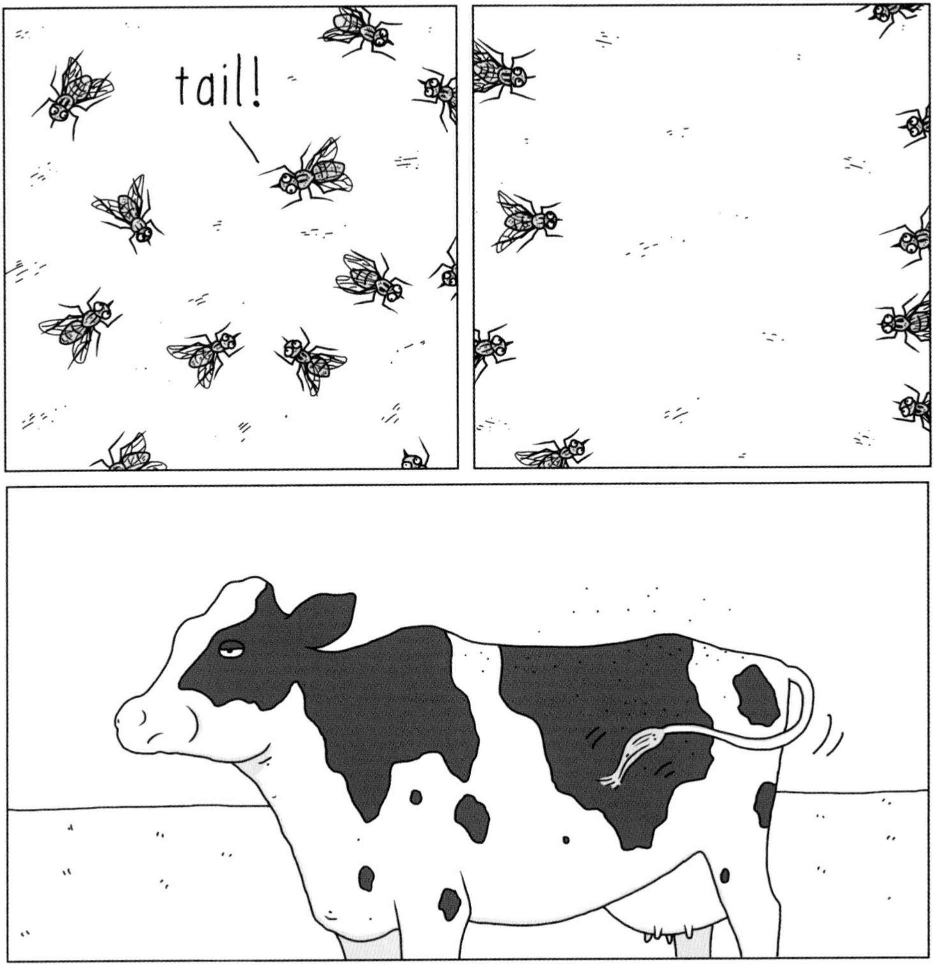
tail!

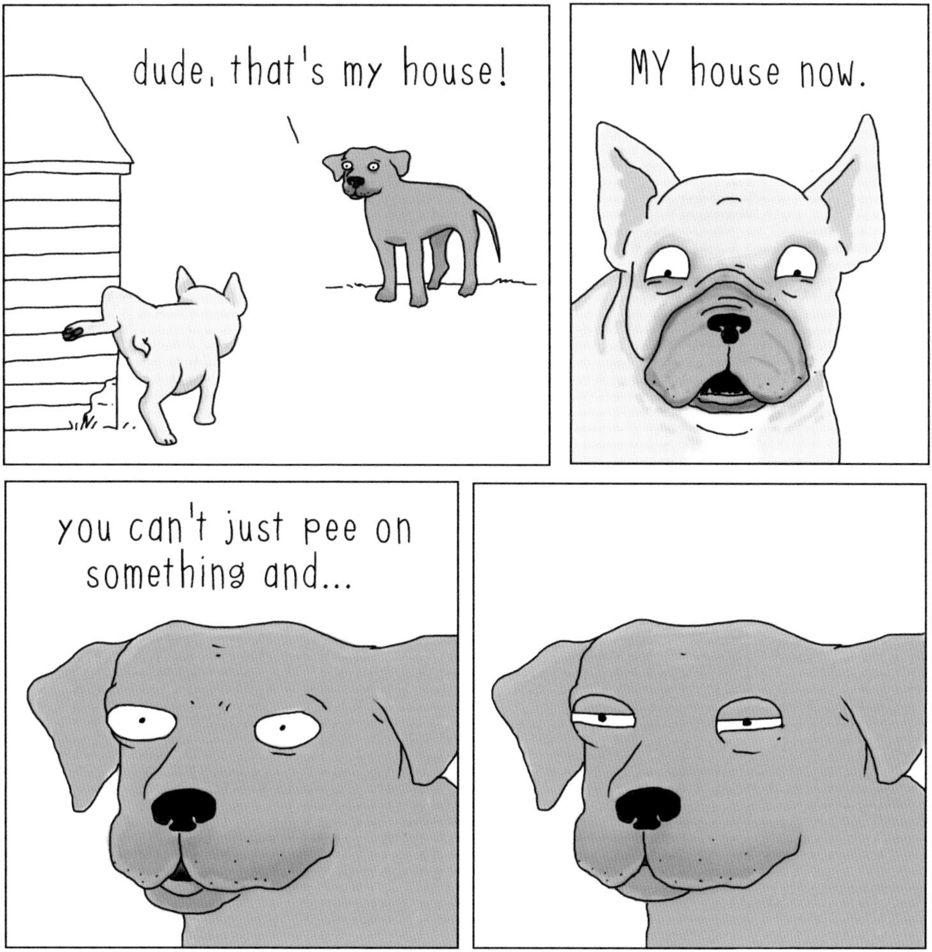
dude, that's my house!
MY house now.
you can't just pee on something and...

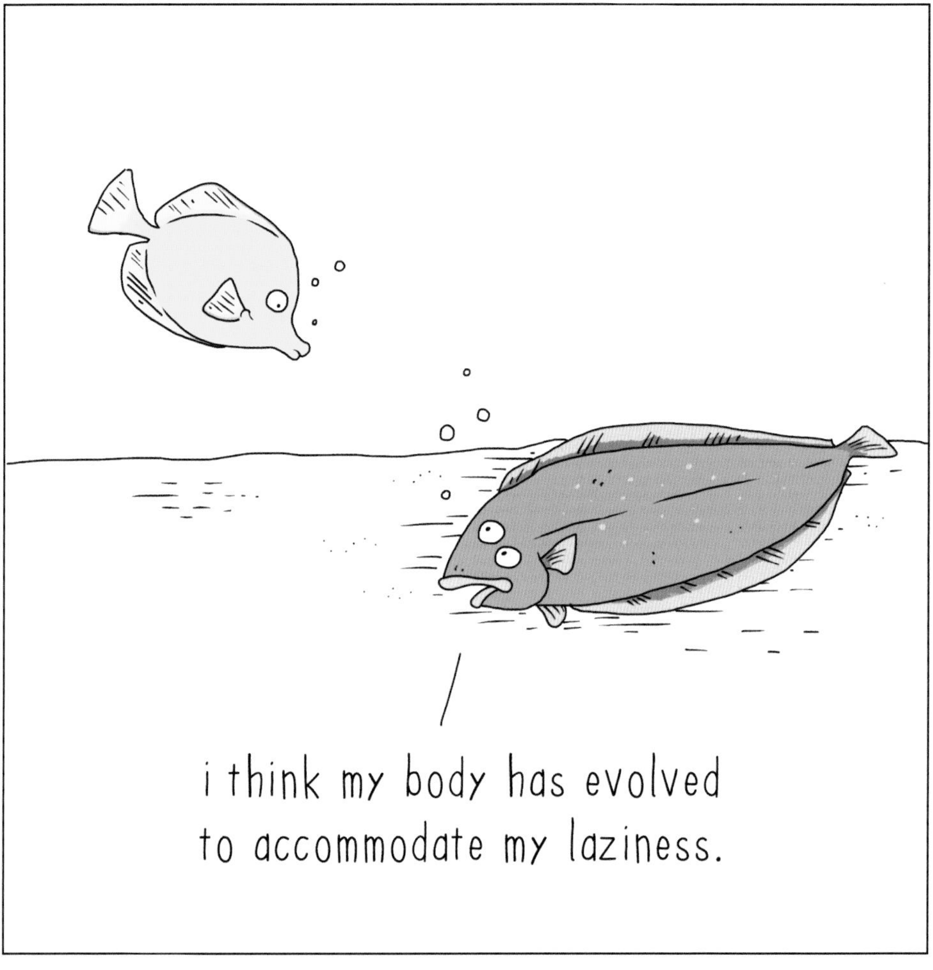
i think my body has evolved
to accommodate my laziness.

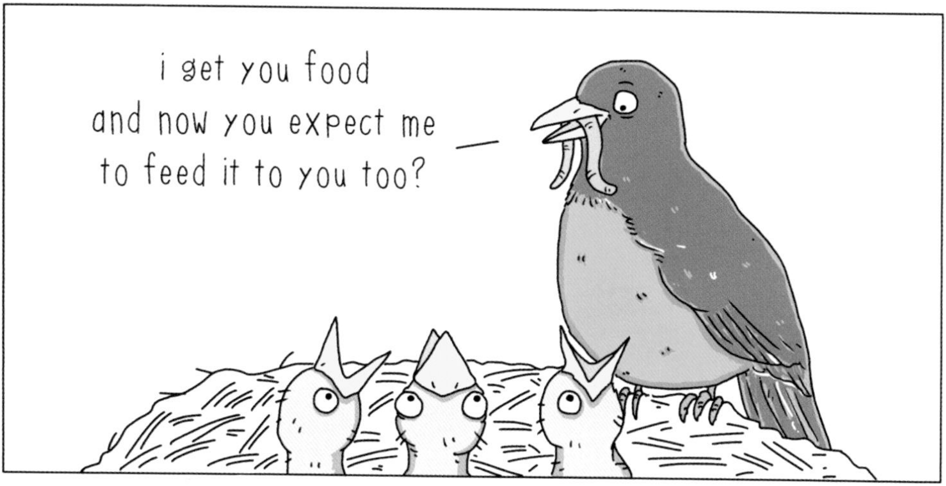
i get you food
and now you expect me
to feed it to you too?

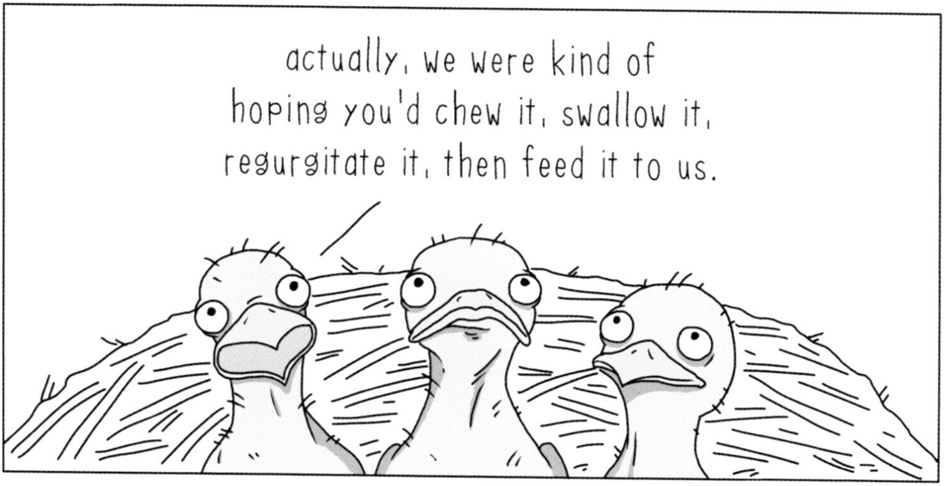
actually, we were kind of
hoping you'd chew it, swallow it,
regurgitate it, then feed it to us.

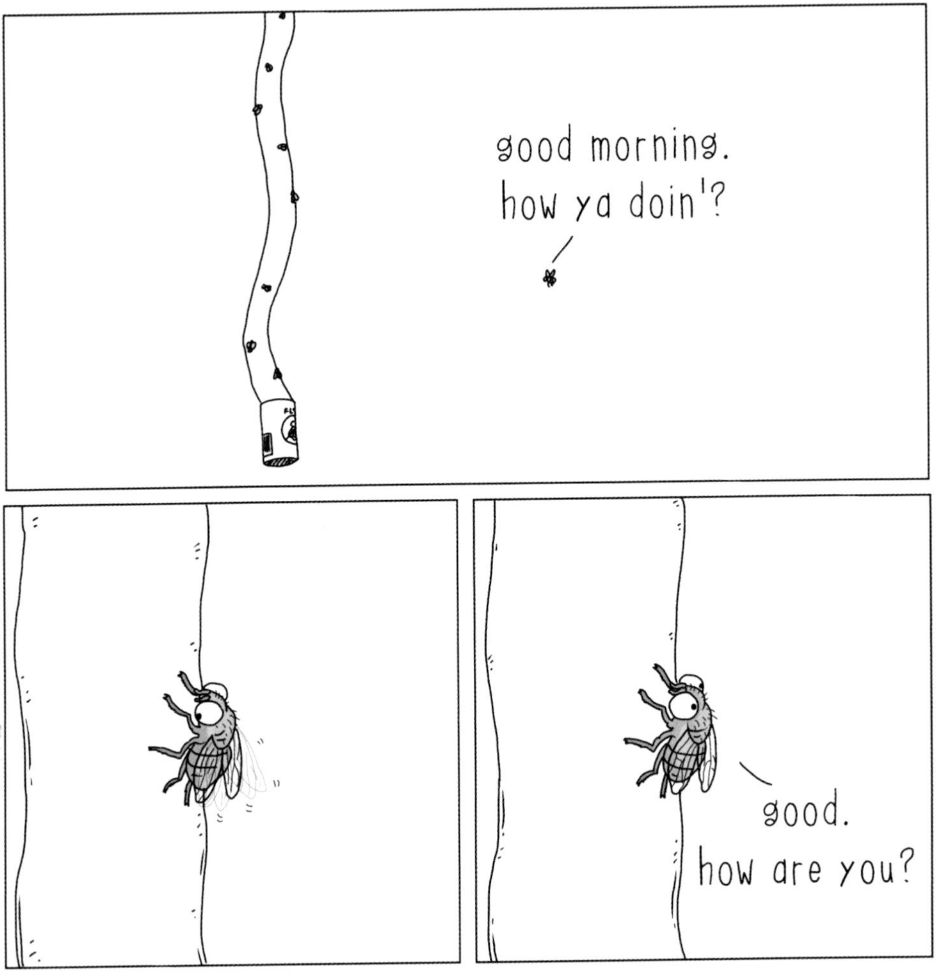
good morning.
how ya doin'?
good.
how are you?

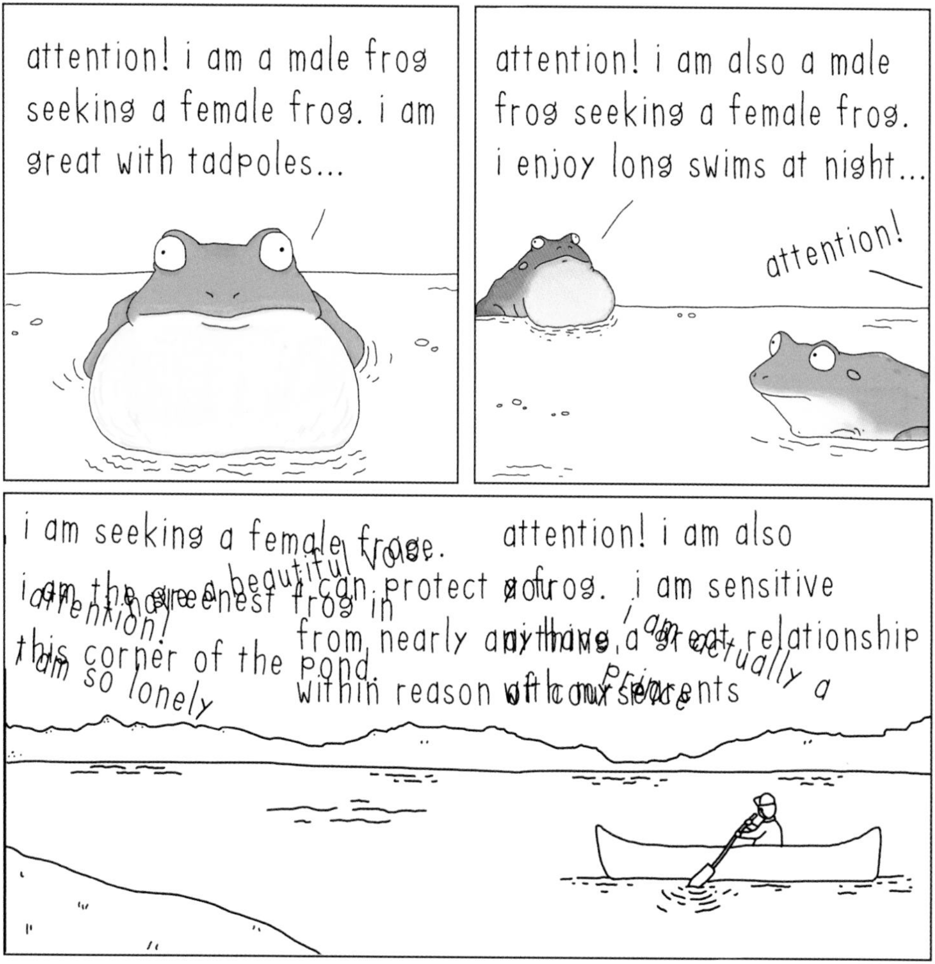
attention! i am a male frog seeking a female frog. i am great with tadpoles...
attention! i am also a male frog seeking a female frog. i enjoy long swims at night...
attention!
i am seeking a female frog.
i am the greenest frog in this corner of the pond.
attention!
i am so lonely
beautiful voice
i can protect you from nearly anything within reason of course
attention! i am also a frog. i am sensitive
i have a great relationship with my parents
i am actually a princess

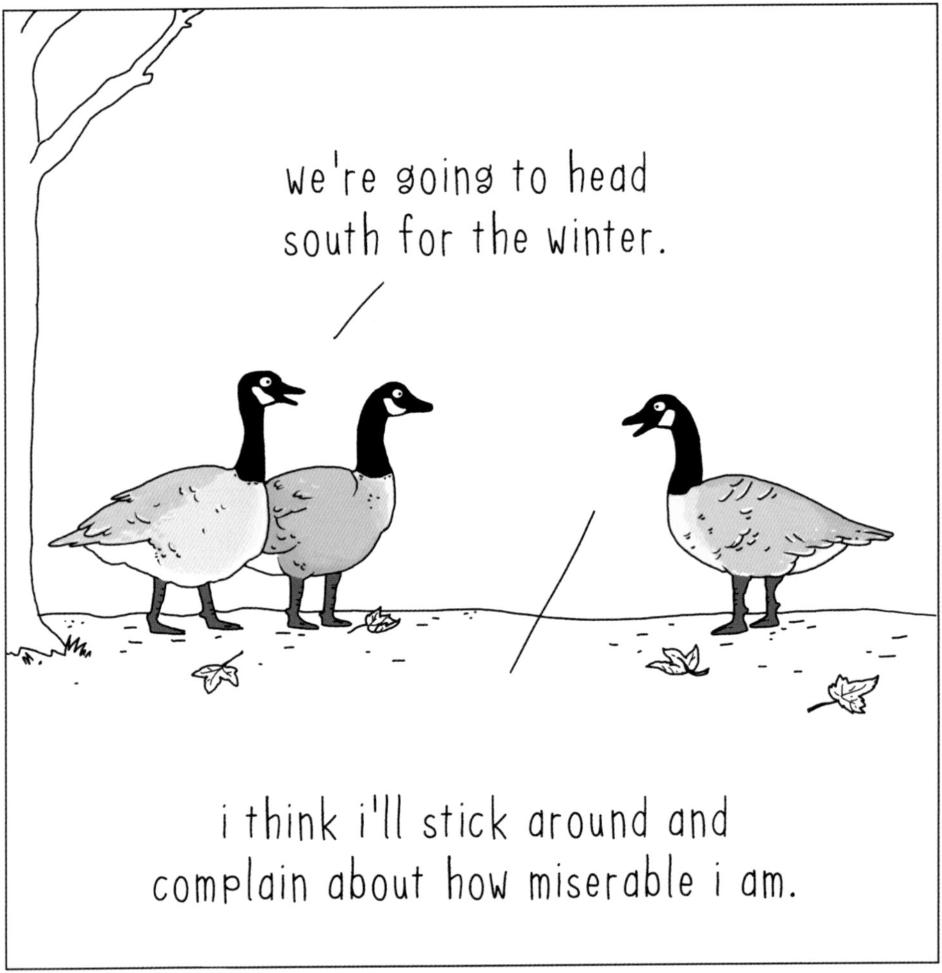
we're going to head south for the winter.
i think i'll stick around and complain about how miserable i am.

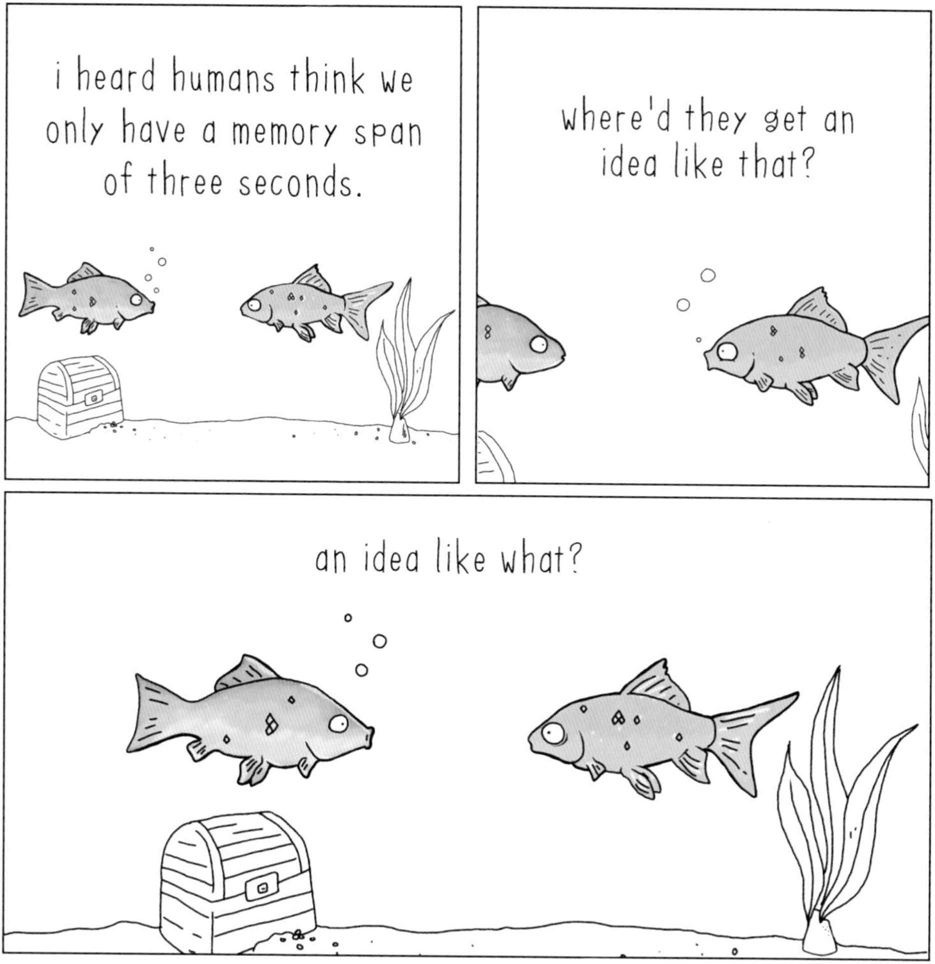
i heard humans think we only have a memory span of three seconds.
where'd they get an idea like that?
an idea like what?

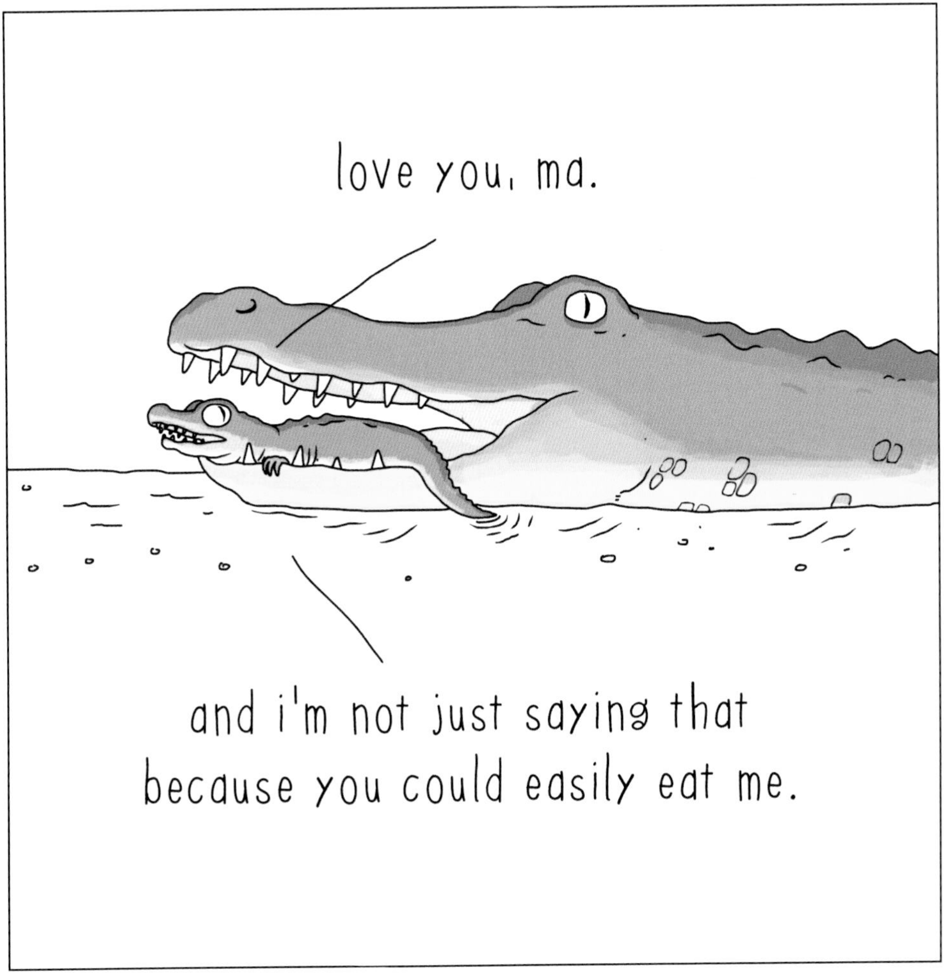
love you, ma.
and i'm not just saying that because you could easily eat me.

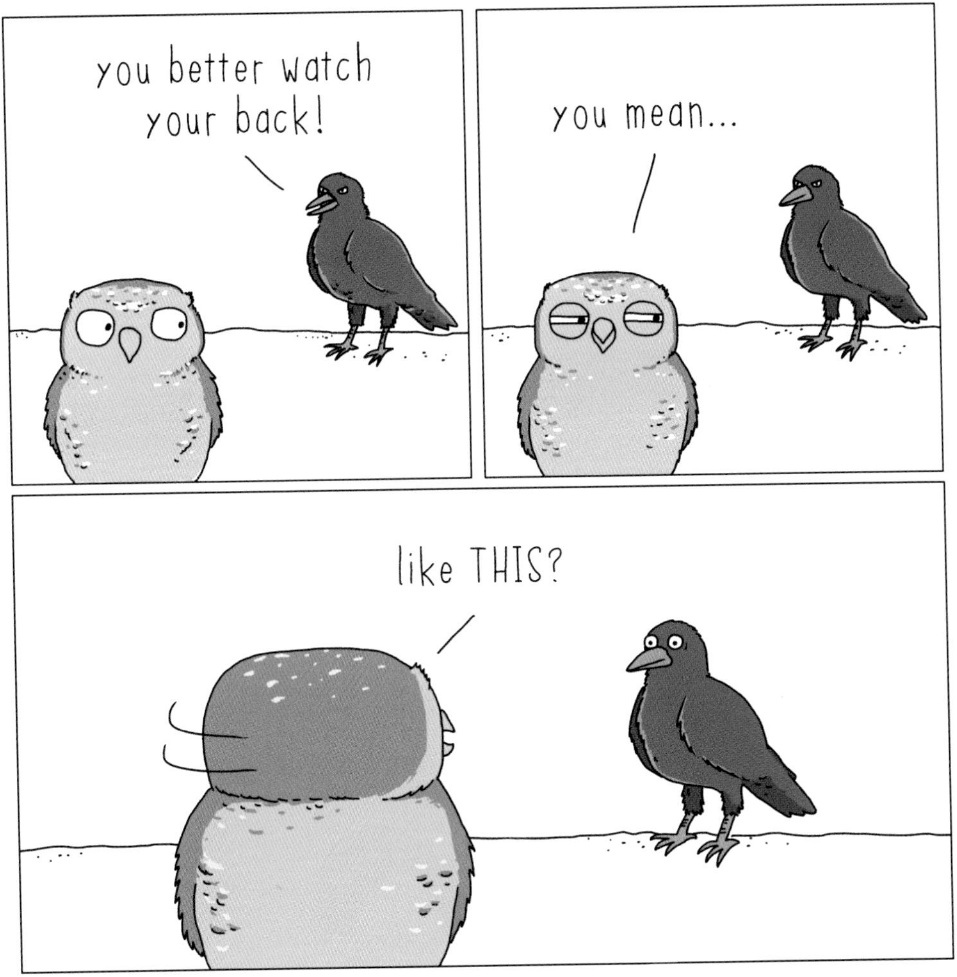
you better watch your back!
you mean...
like THIS?

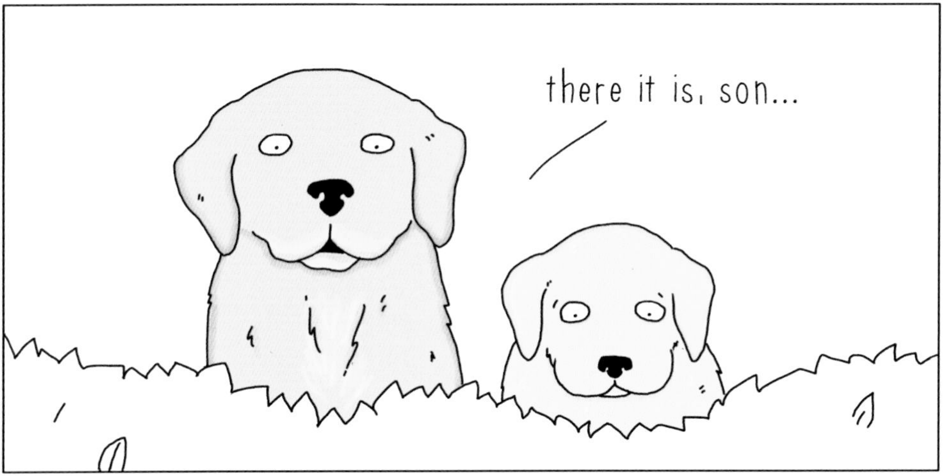
there it is, son...

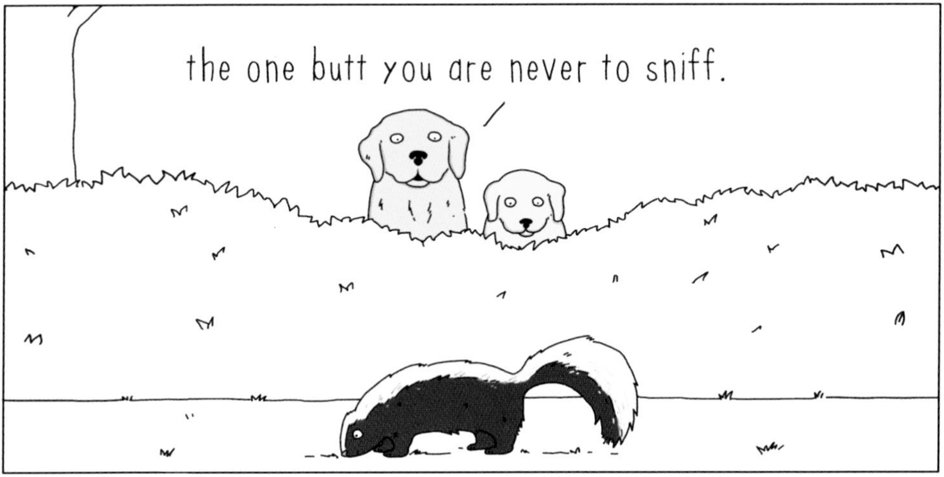
the one butt you are never to sniff.

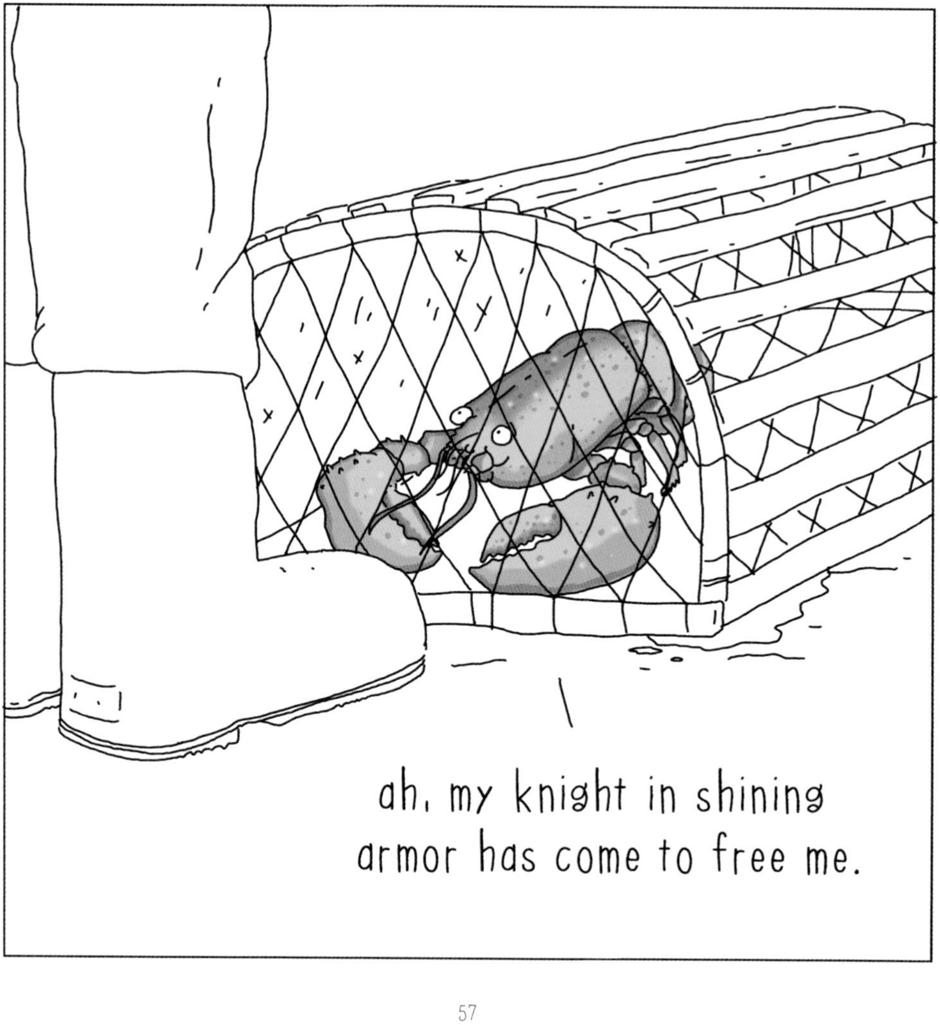

ah, my knight in shining
armor has come to free me.

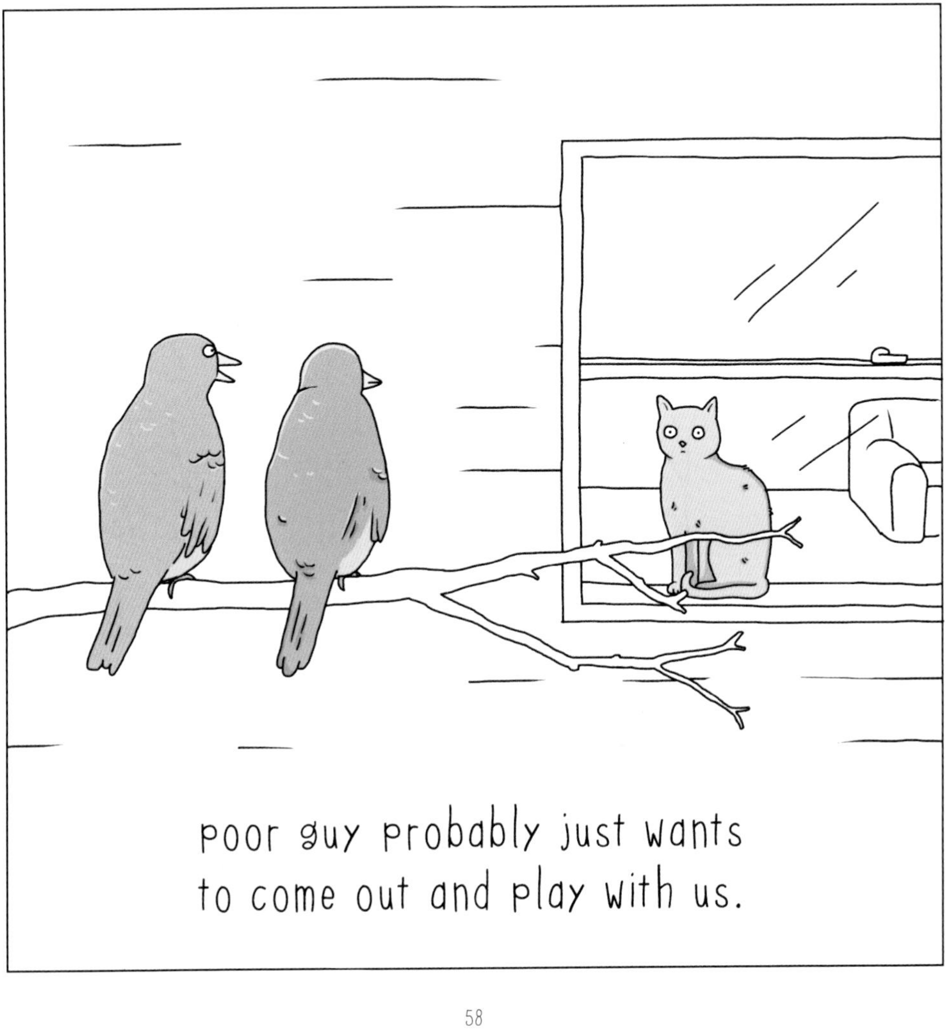

poor guy probably just wants
to come out and play with us.

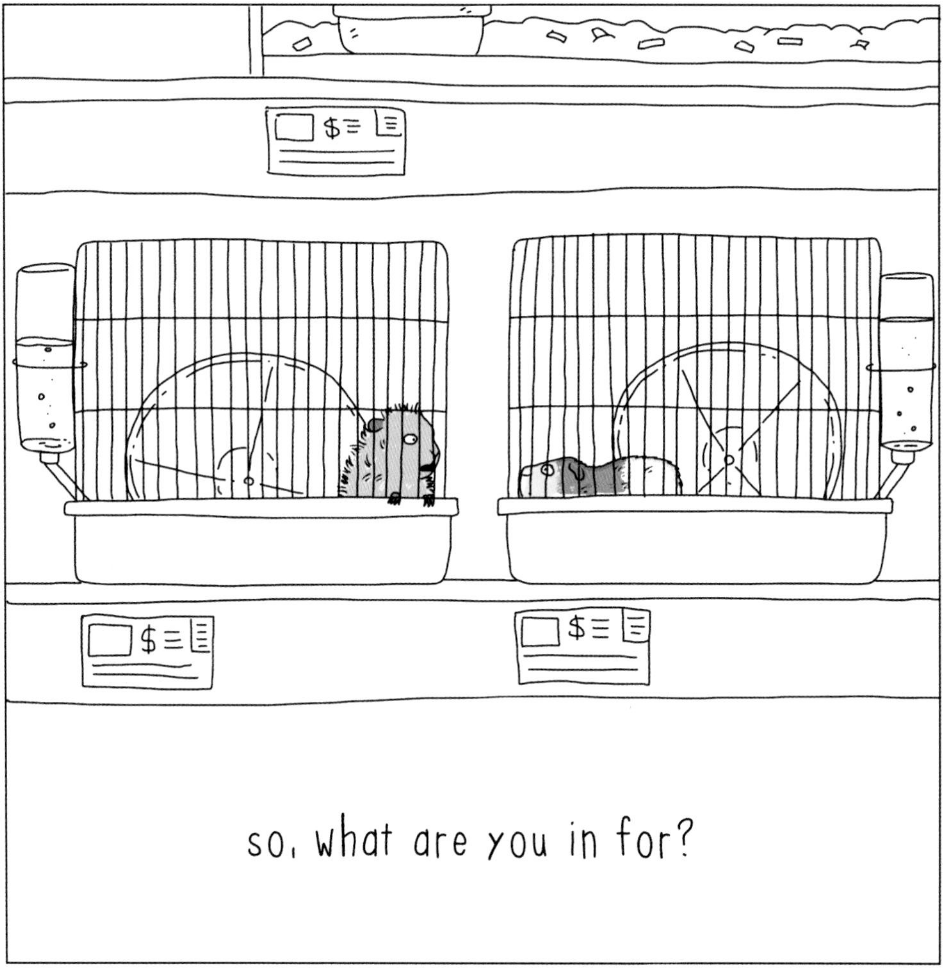
so, what are you in for?

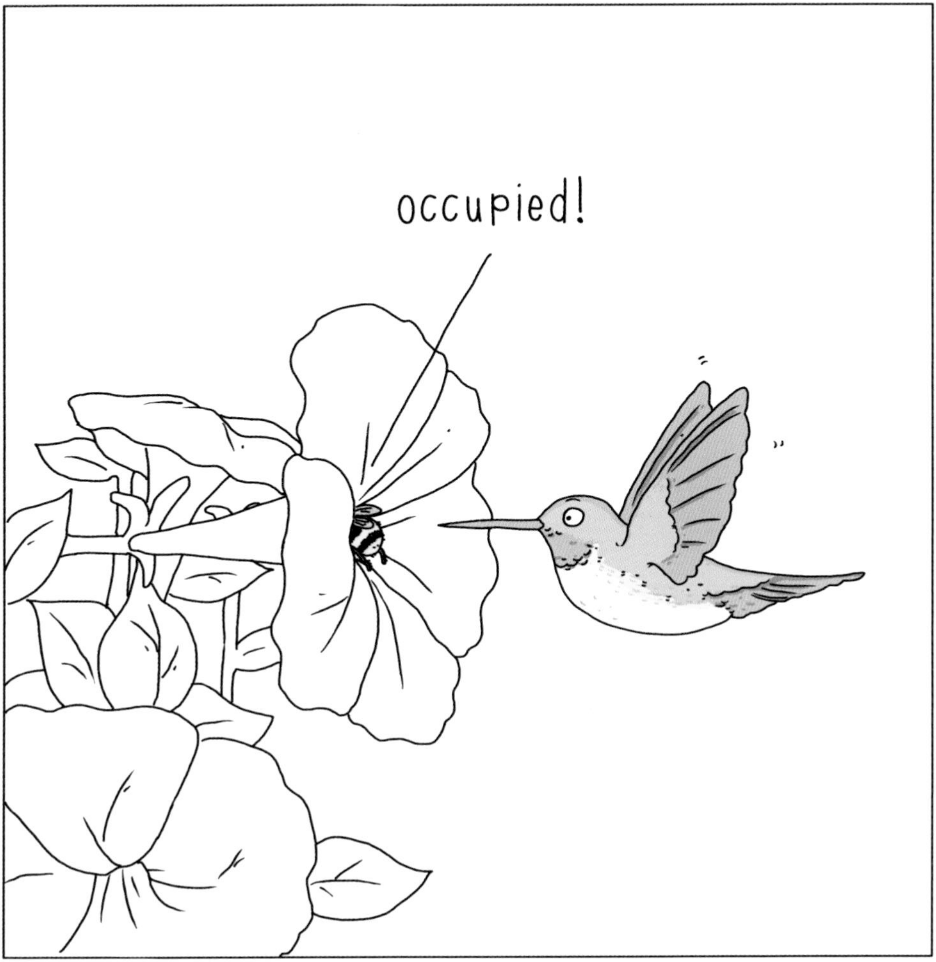
occupied!

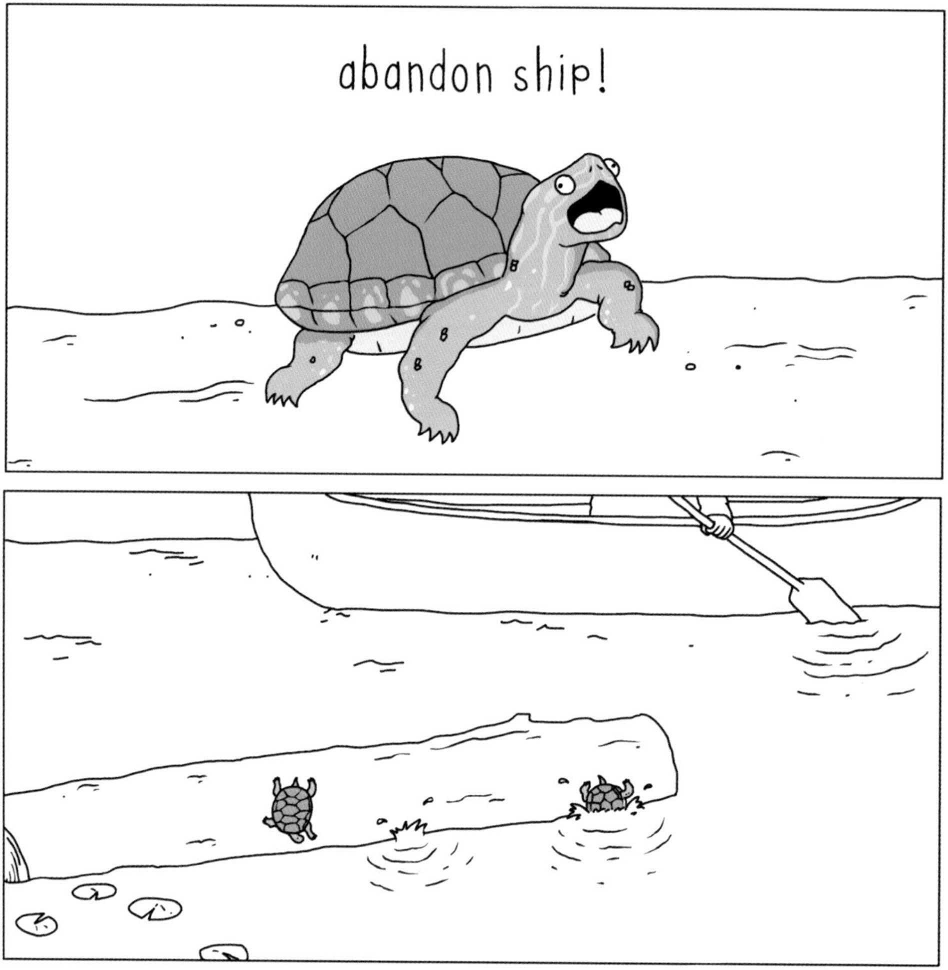
abandon ship!

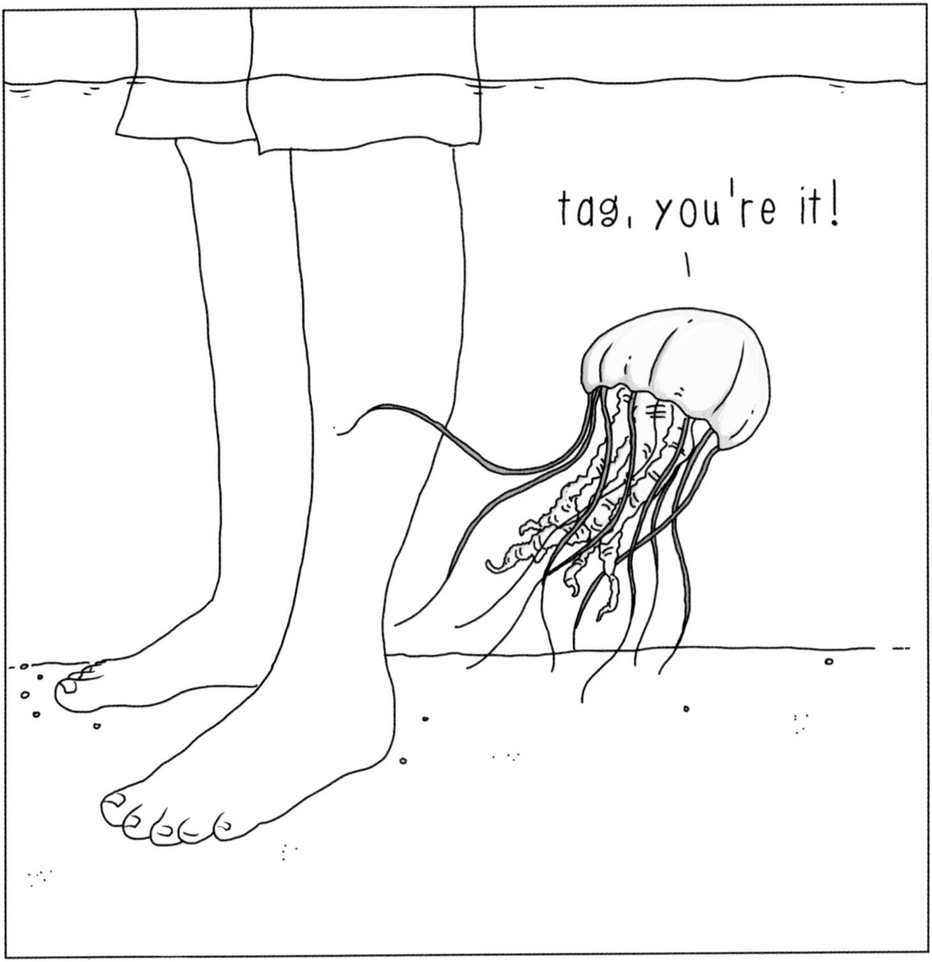
tag, you're it!

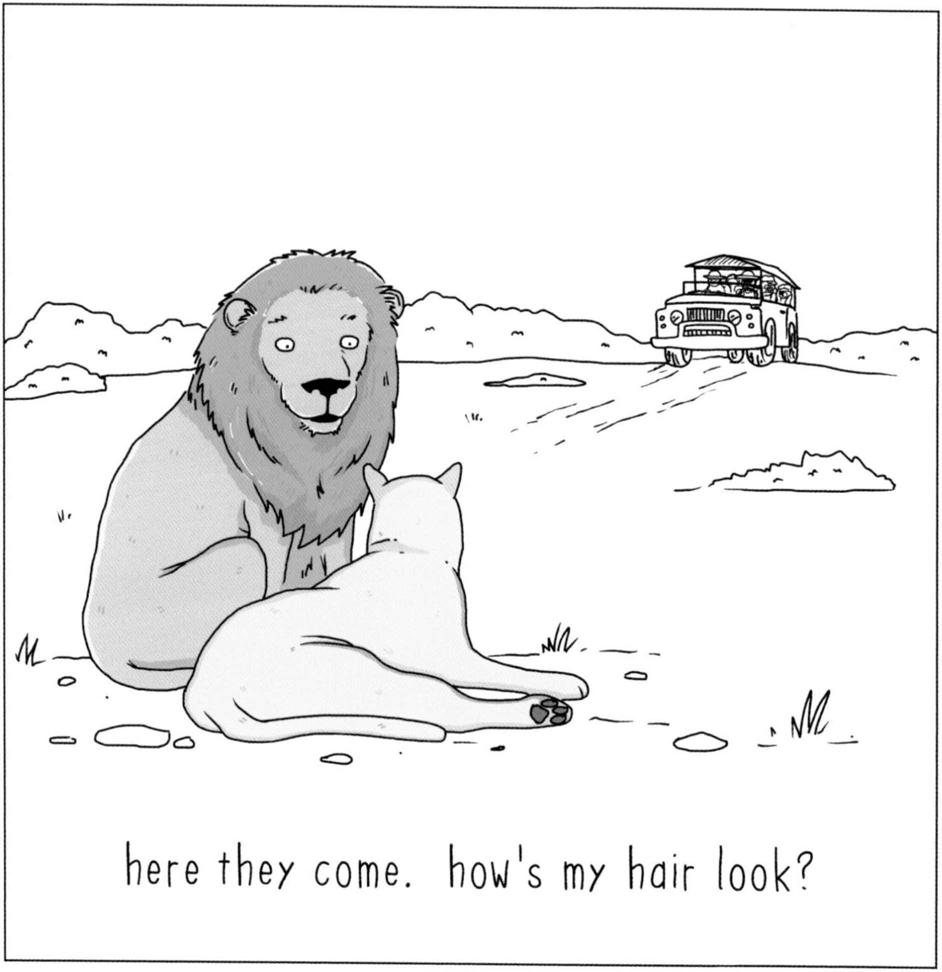
here they come. how's my hair look?

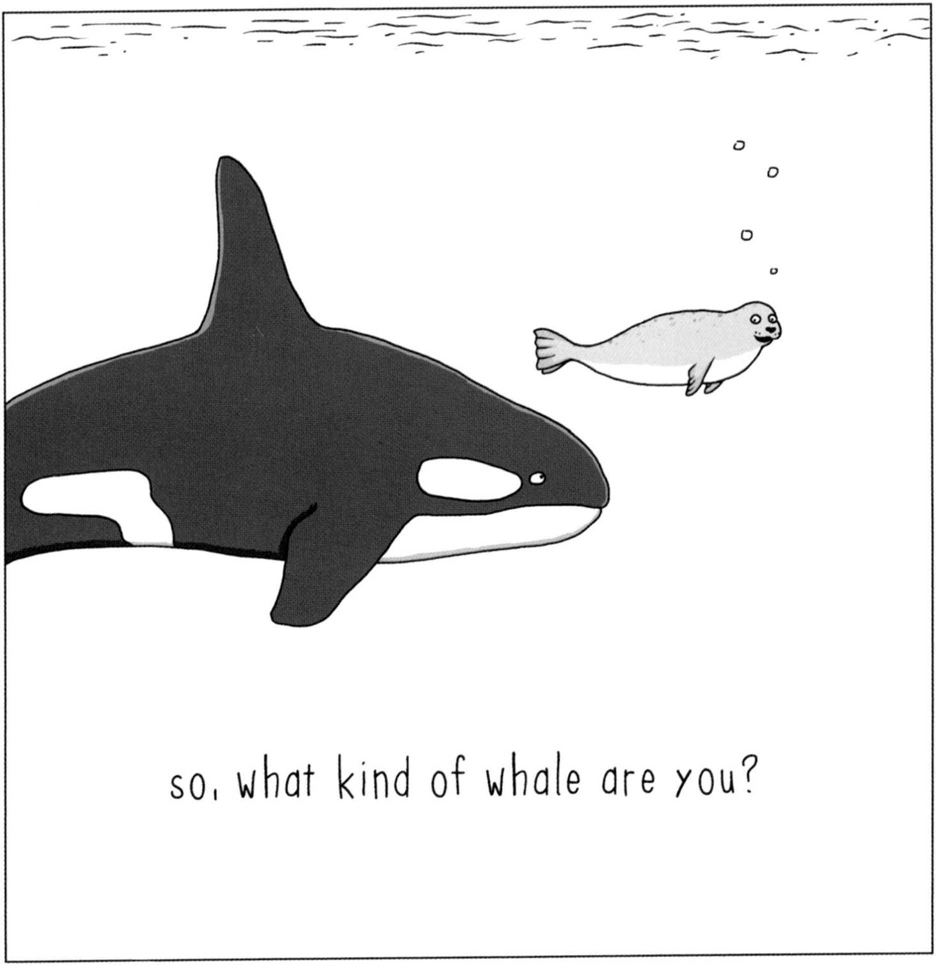
so, what kind of whale are you?

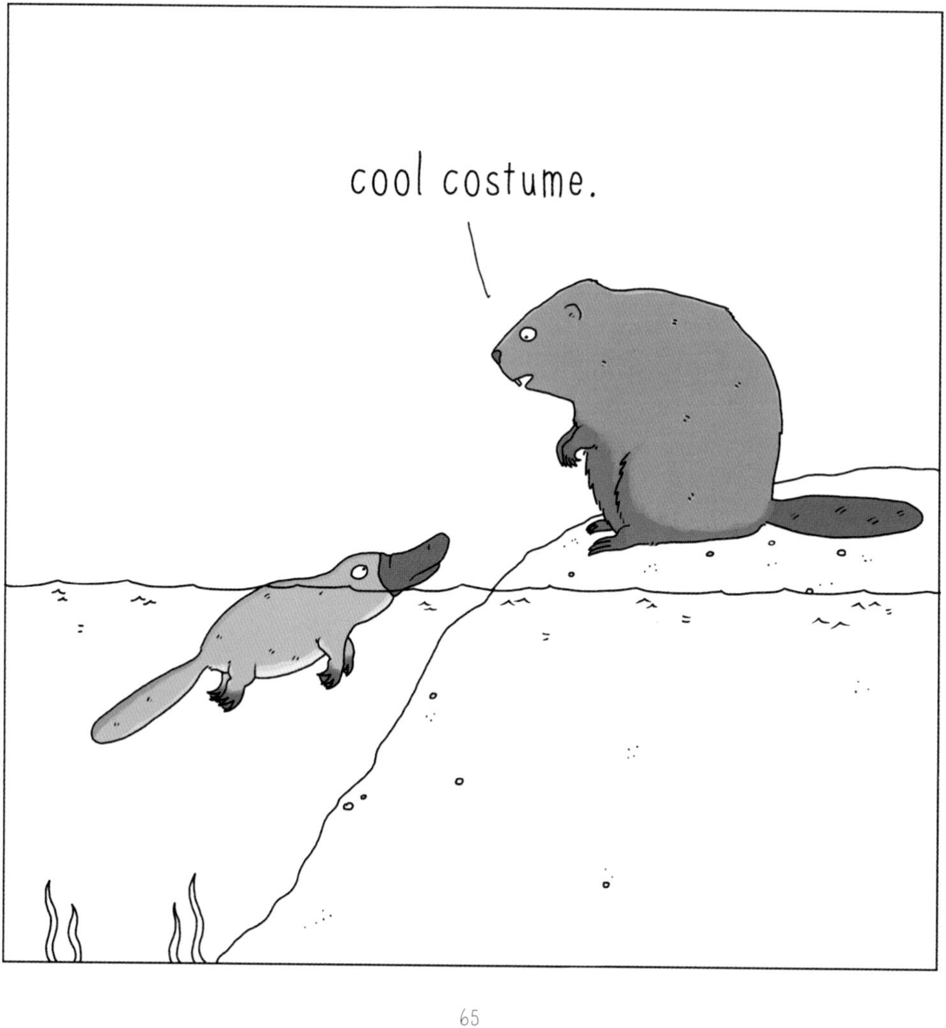
cool costume.

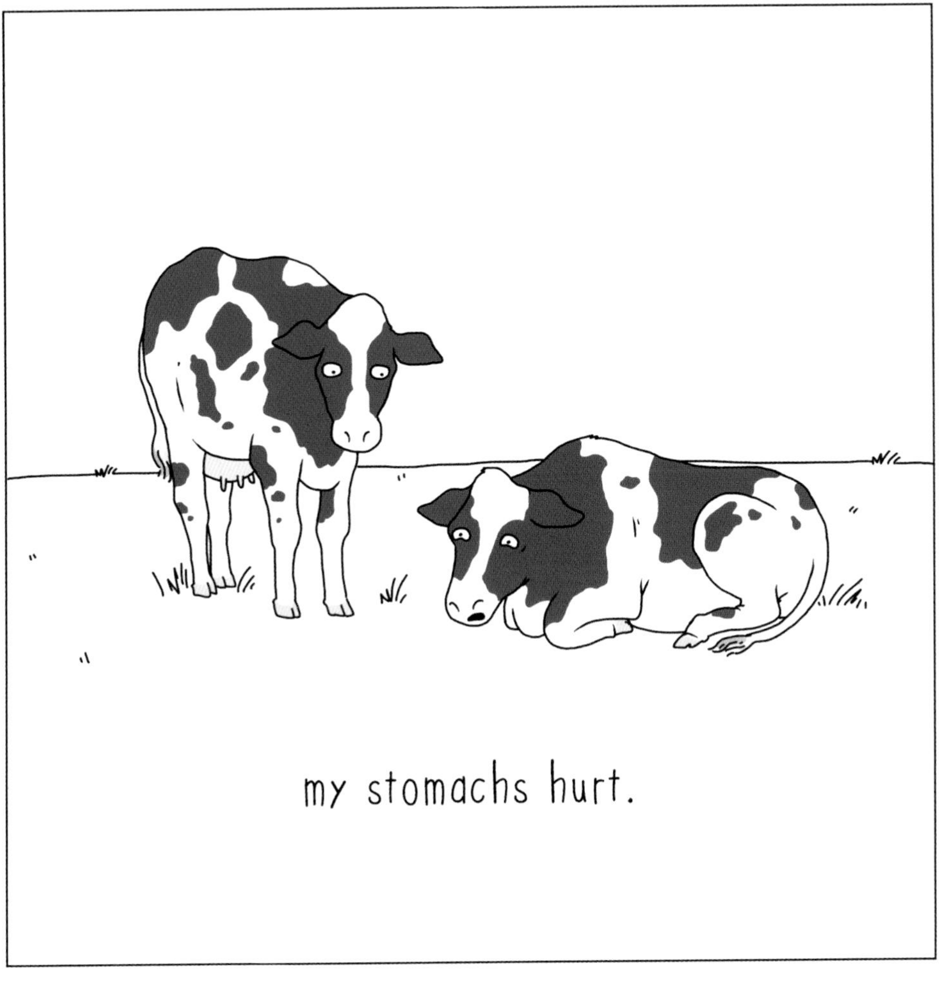
my stomachs hurt.

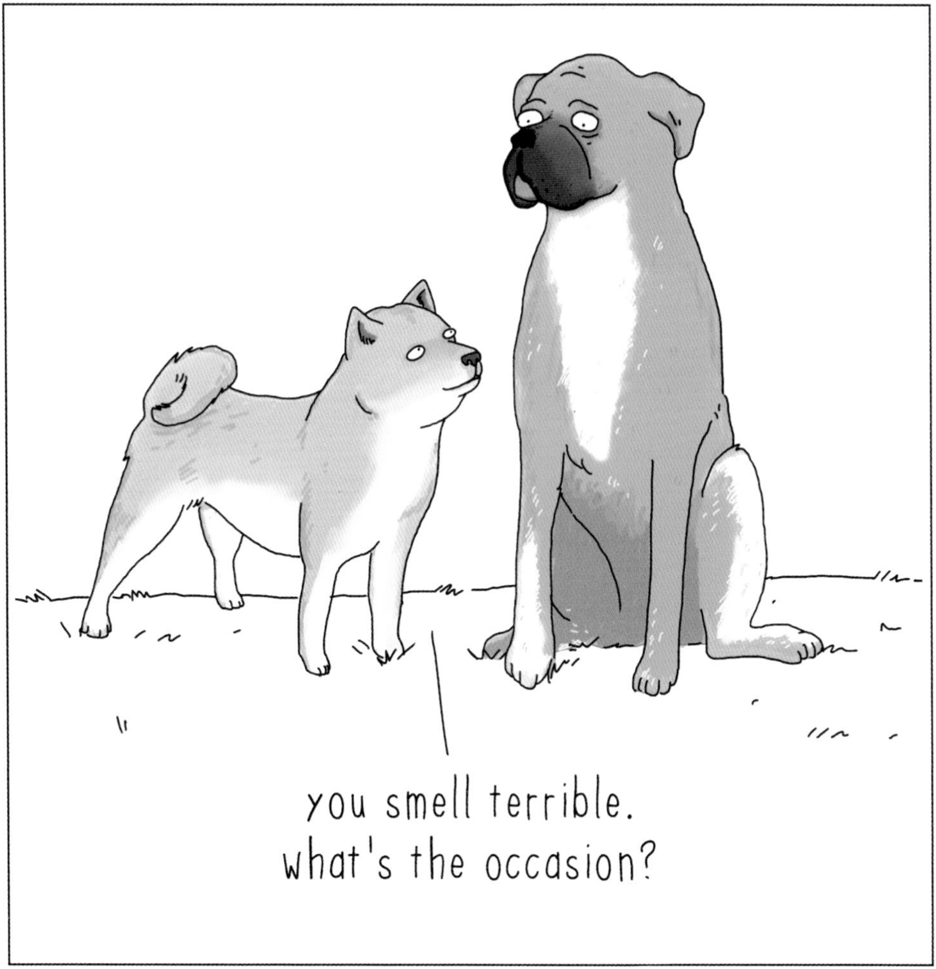
you smell terrible.
what's the occasion?

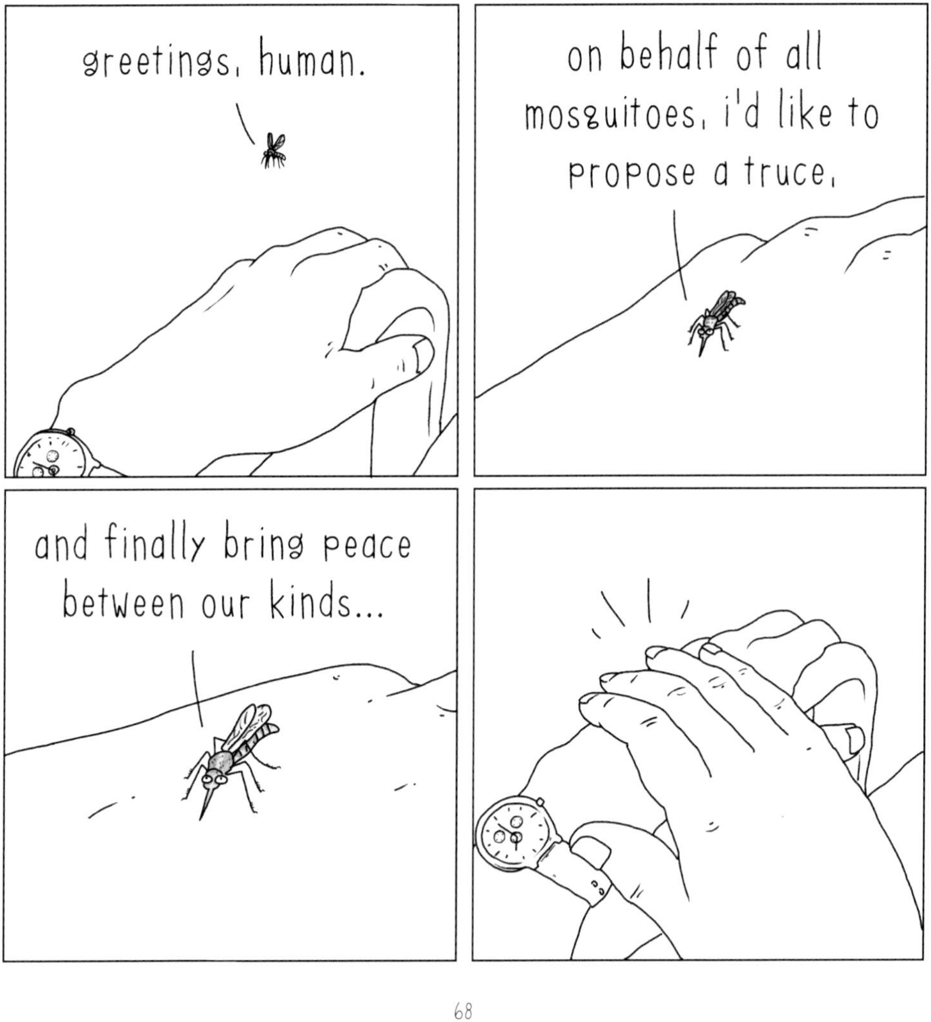
greetings, human.
on behalf of all mosquitoes, i'd like to propose a truce.
and finally bring peace between our kinds...

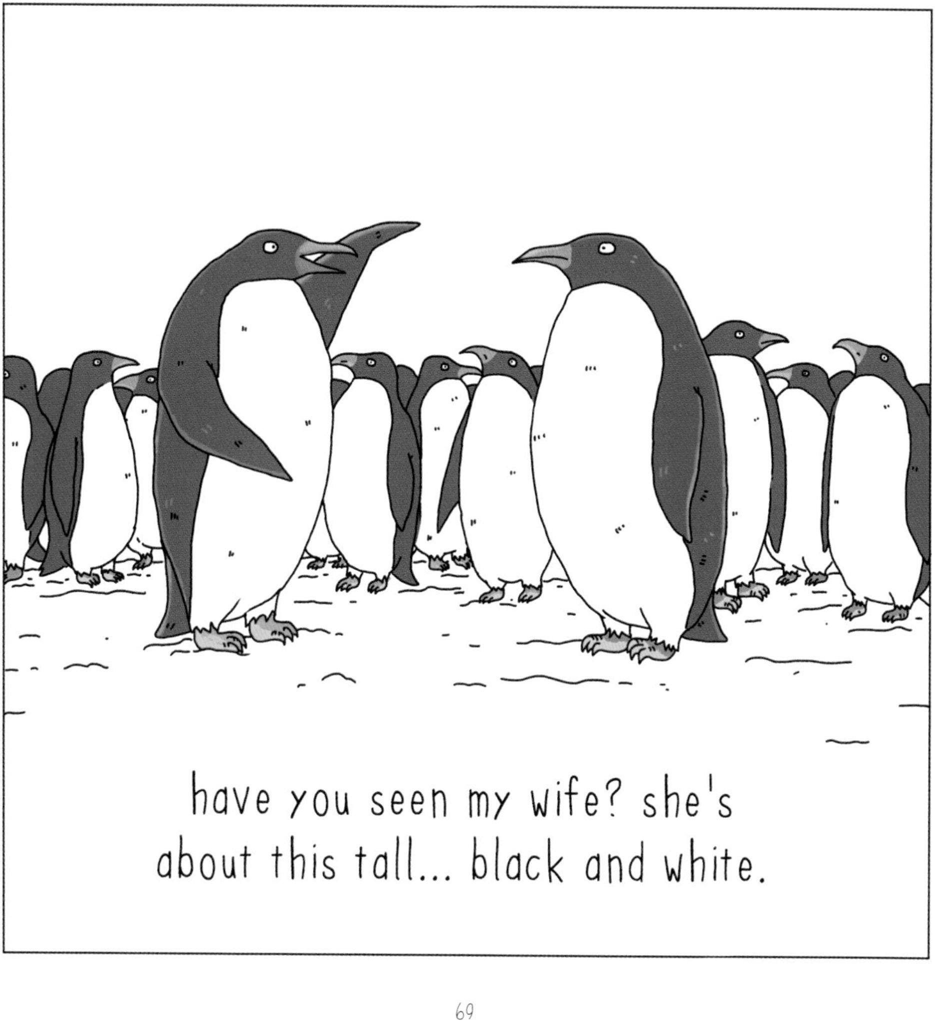

have you seen my wife? she's
about this tall... black and white.

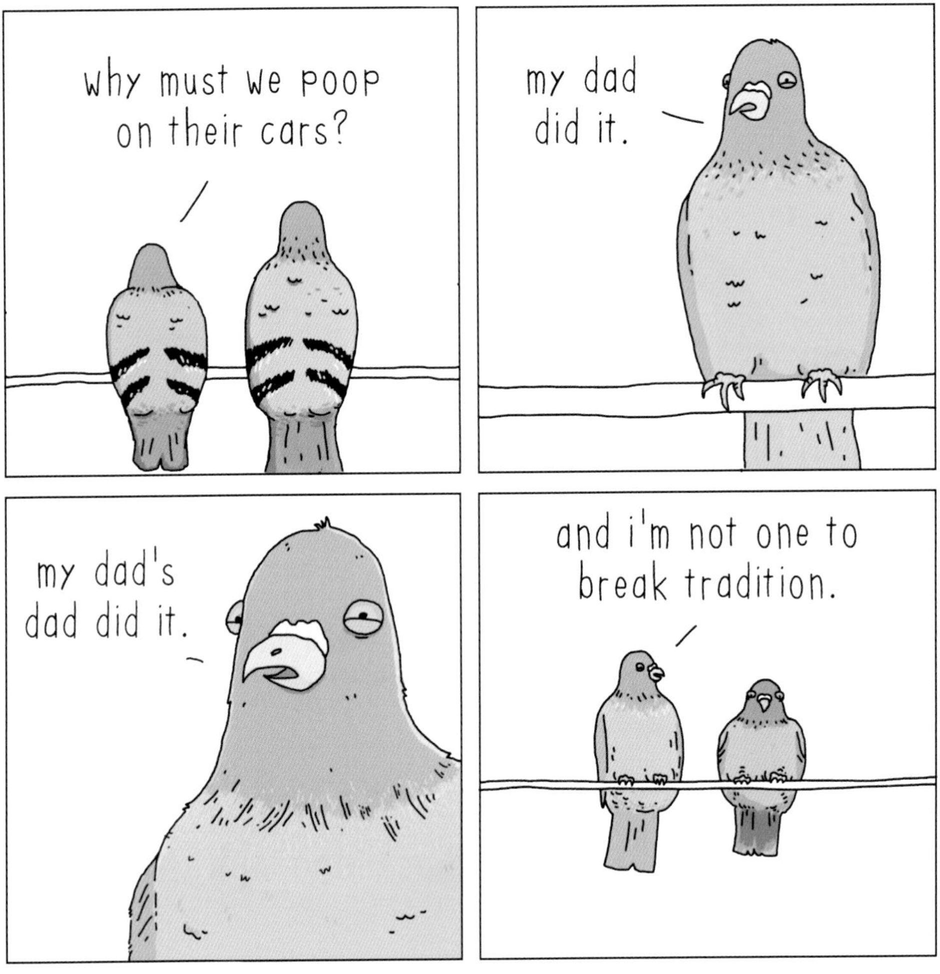
why must we poop on their cars?
my dad did it.
my dad's dad did it.
and i'm not one to break tradition.

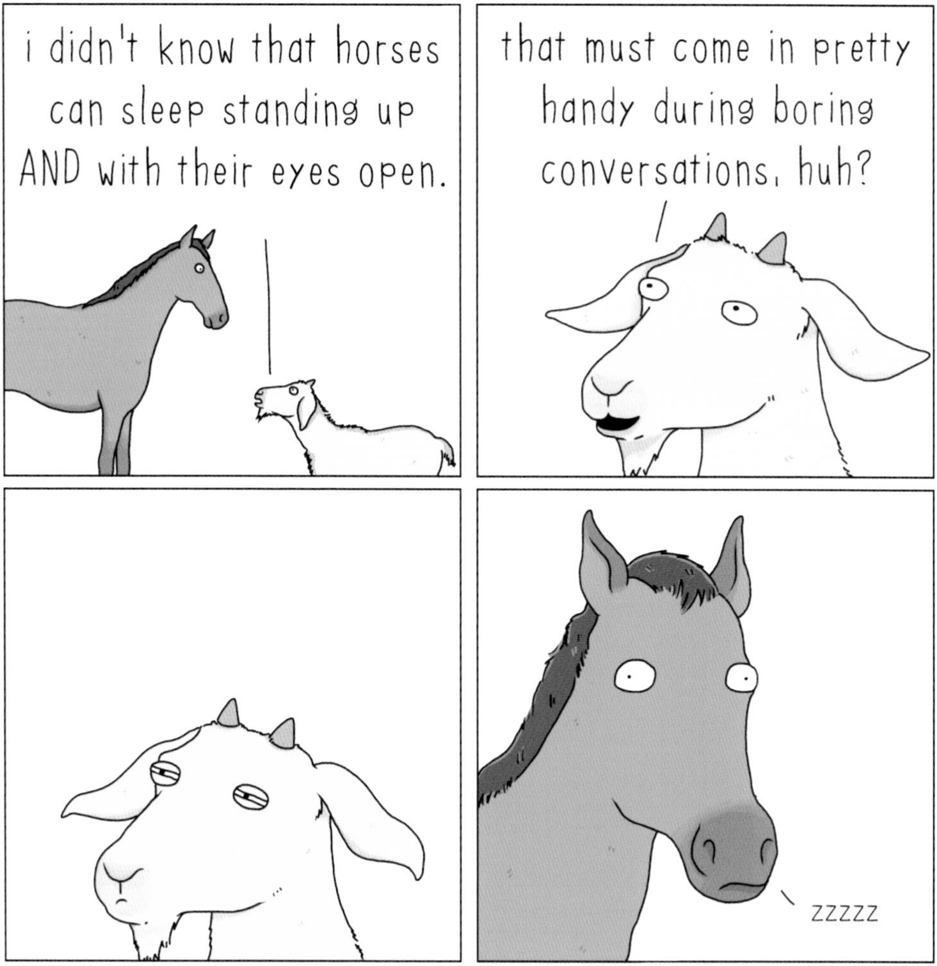
i didn't know that horses can sleep standing up AND with their eyes open.
that must come in pretty handy during boring conversations, huh?
ZZZZZ

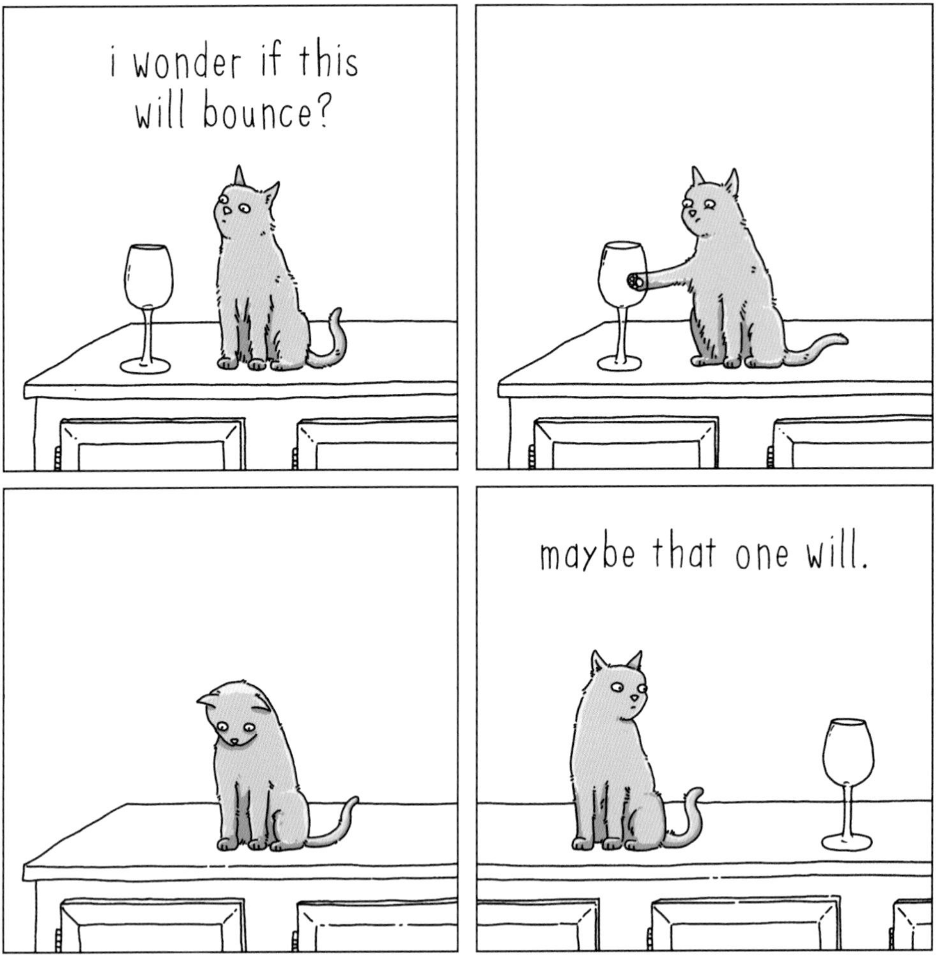
i wonder if this
will bounce?
maybe that one will.

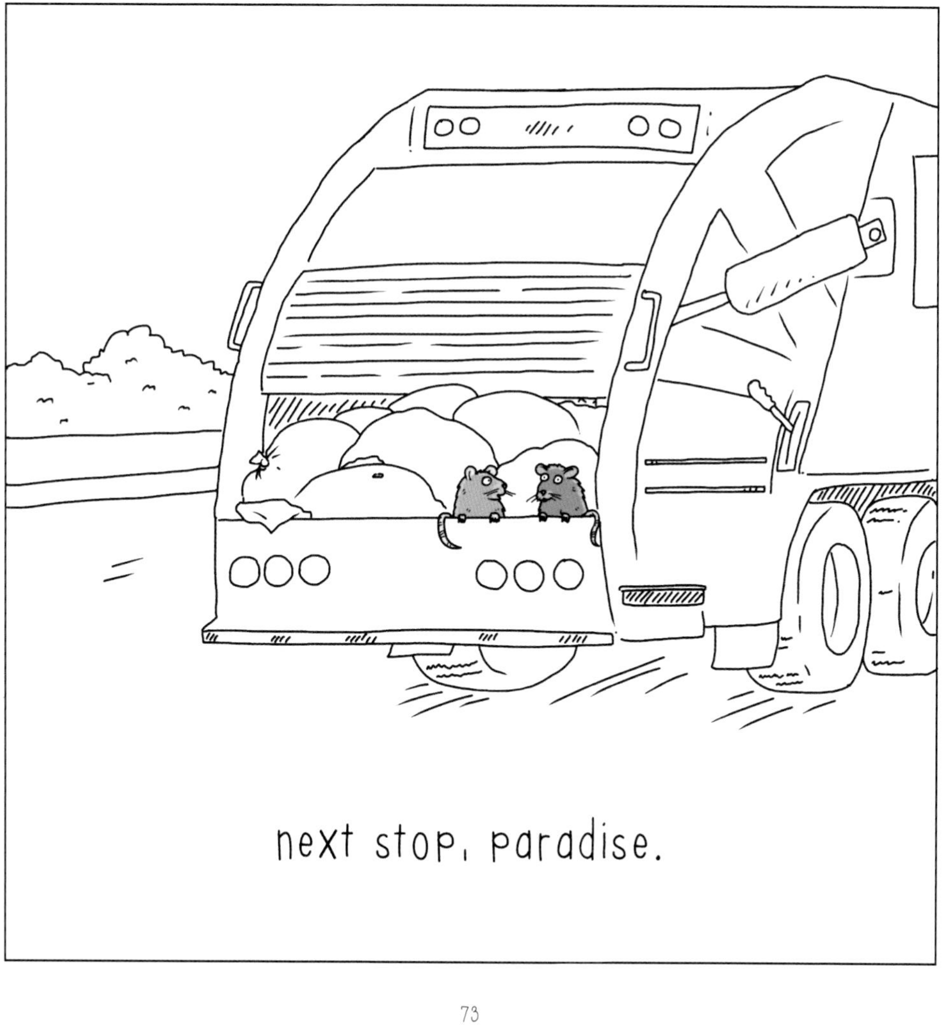

next stop, paradise.

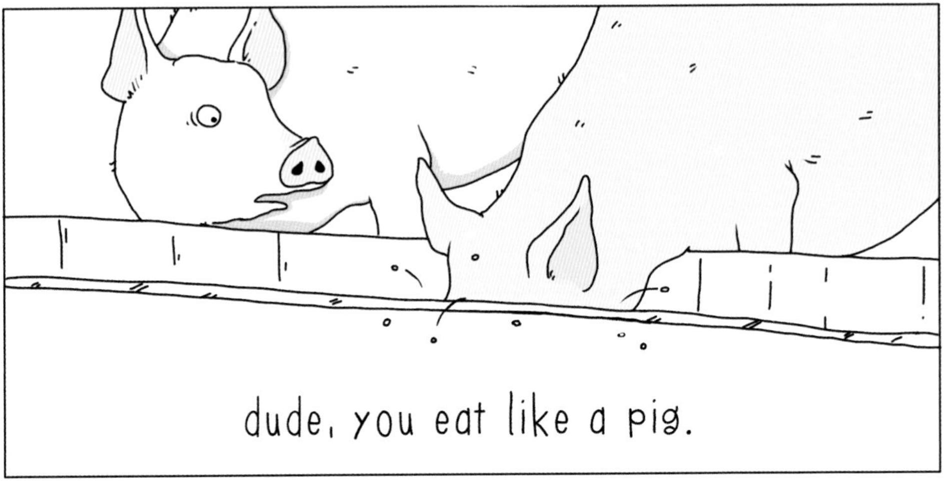
dude, you eat like a pig.

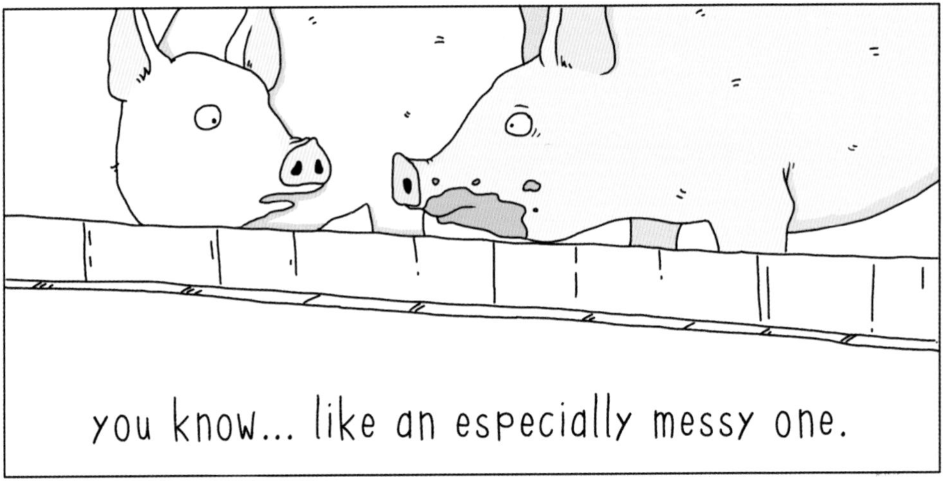
you know... like an especially messy one.

you know you could have
just ridden me here, right?
that's kind of my thing.

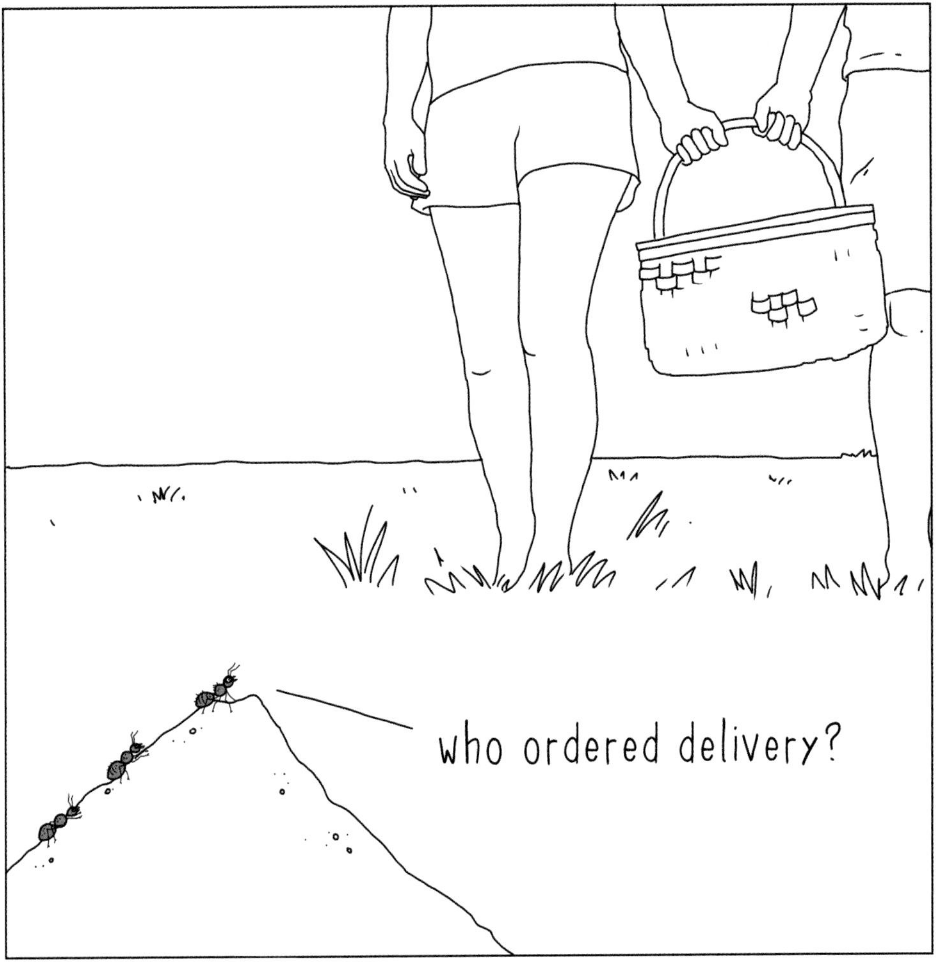
who ordered delivery?

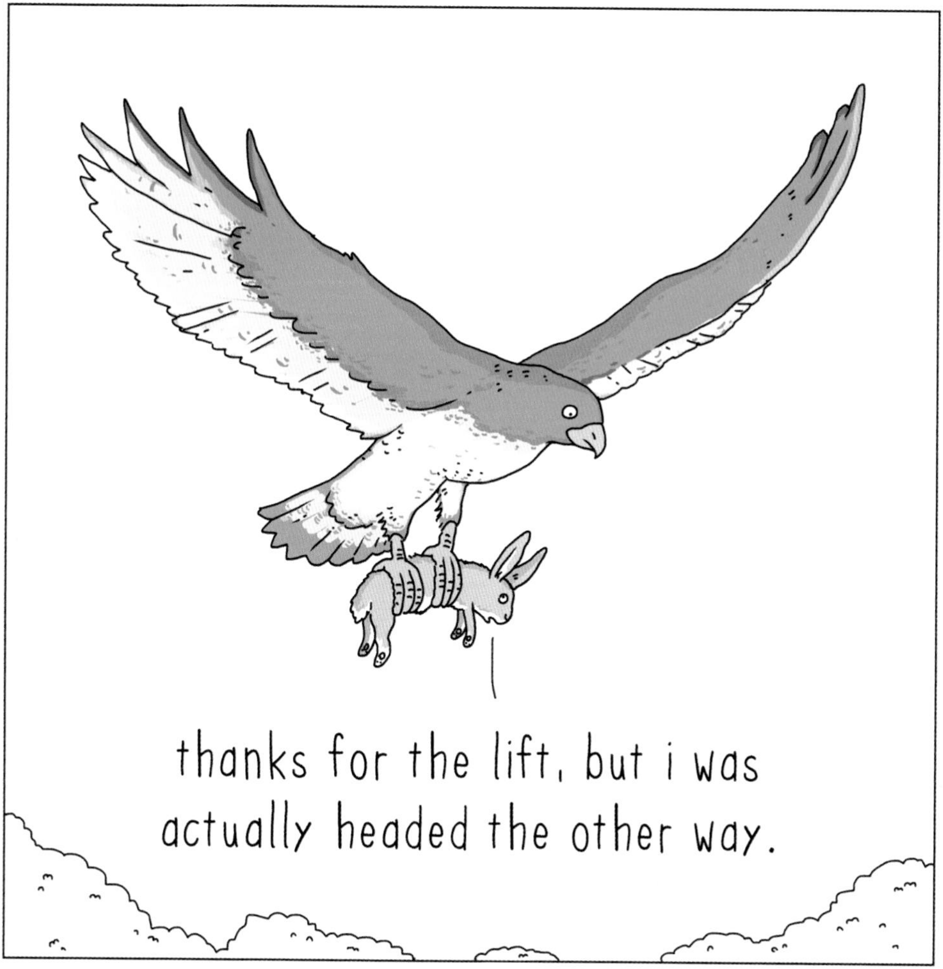
thanks for the lift, but i was
actually headed the other way.

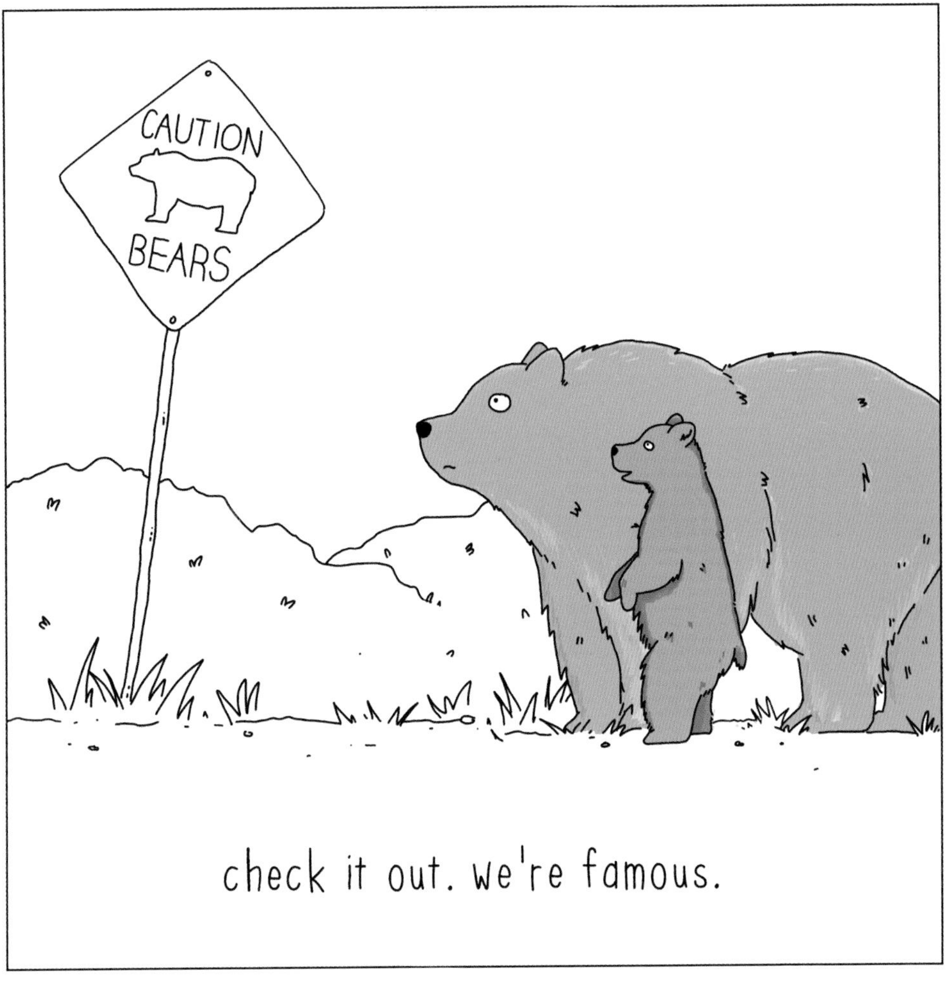
CAUTION
BEARS

check it out. we're famous.

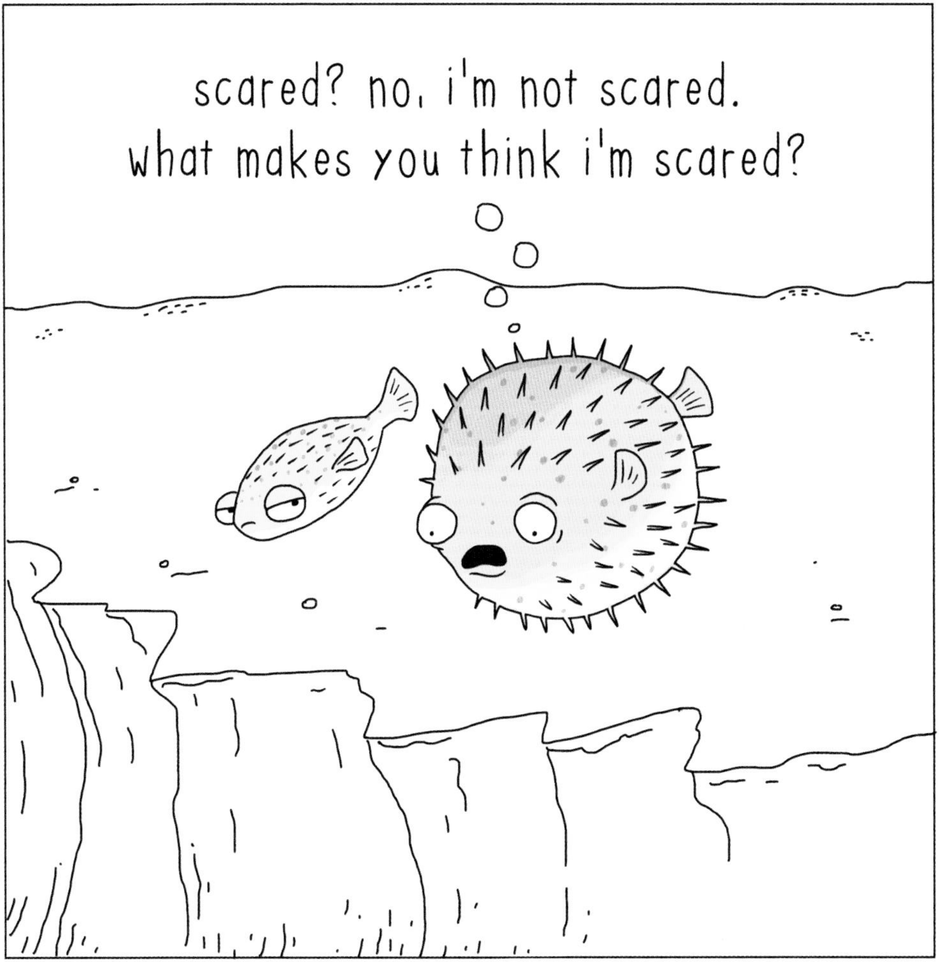
scared? no, i'm not scared.
what makes you think i'm scared?

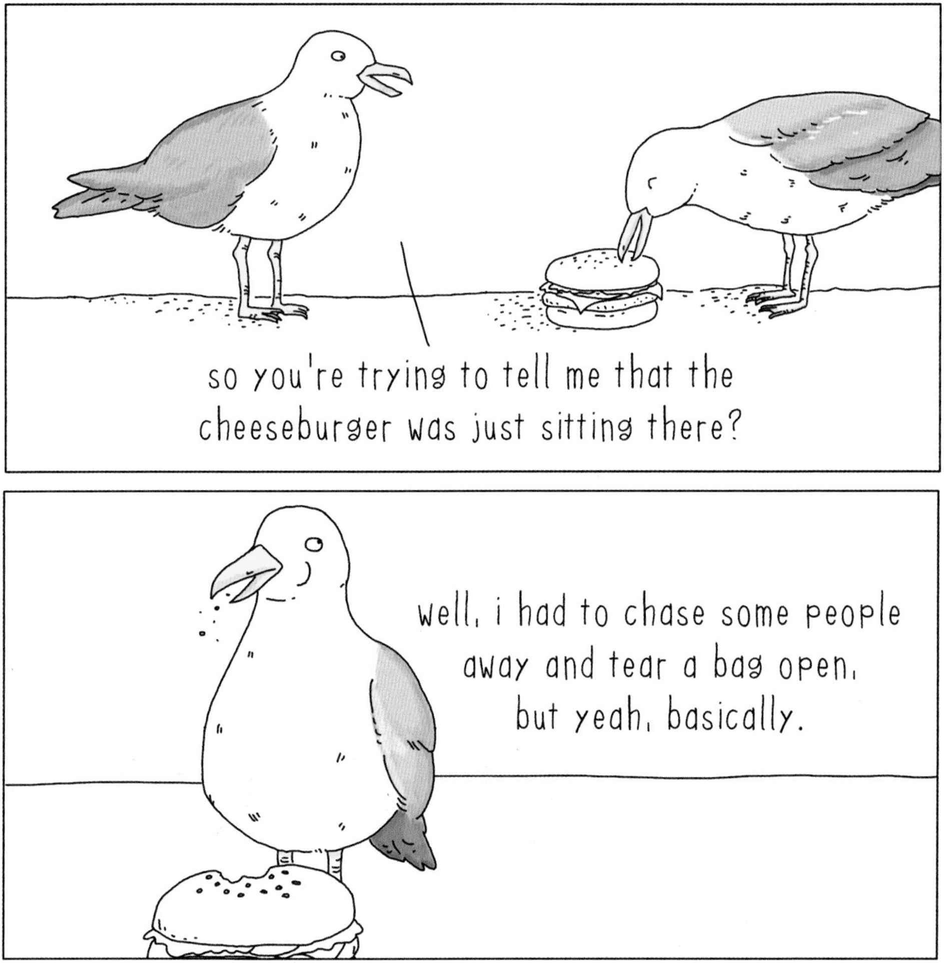
so you're trying to tell me that the cheeseburger was just sitting there?
well, i had to chase some people away and tear a bag open, but yeah, basically.

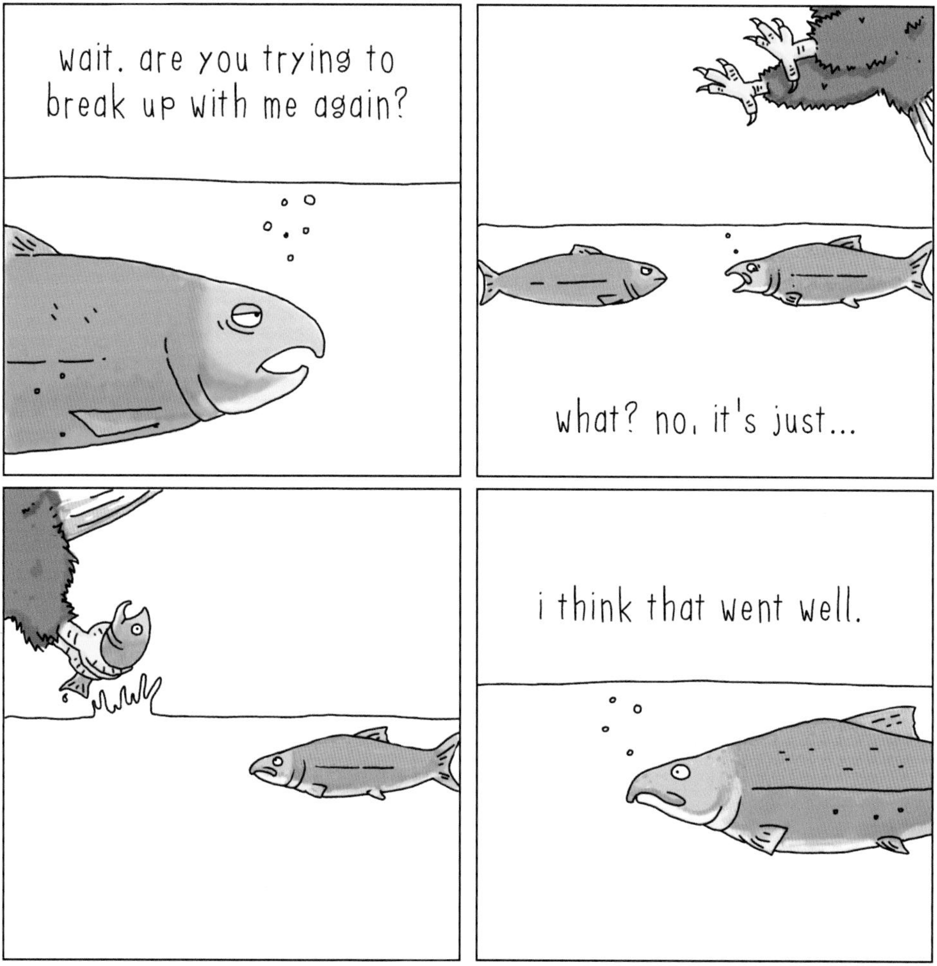
wait. are you trying to break up with me again?
what? no, it's just...
i think that went well.

you're standing on my dinner.

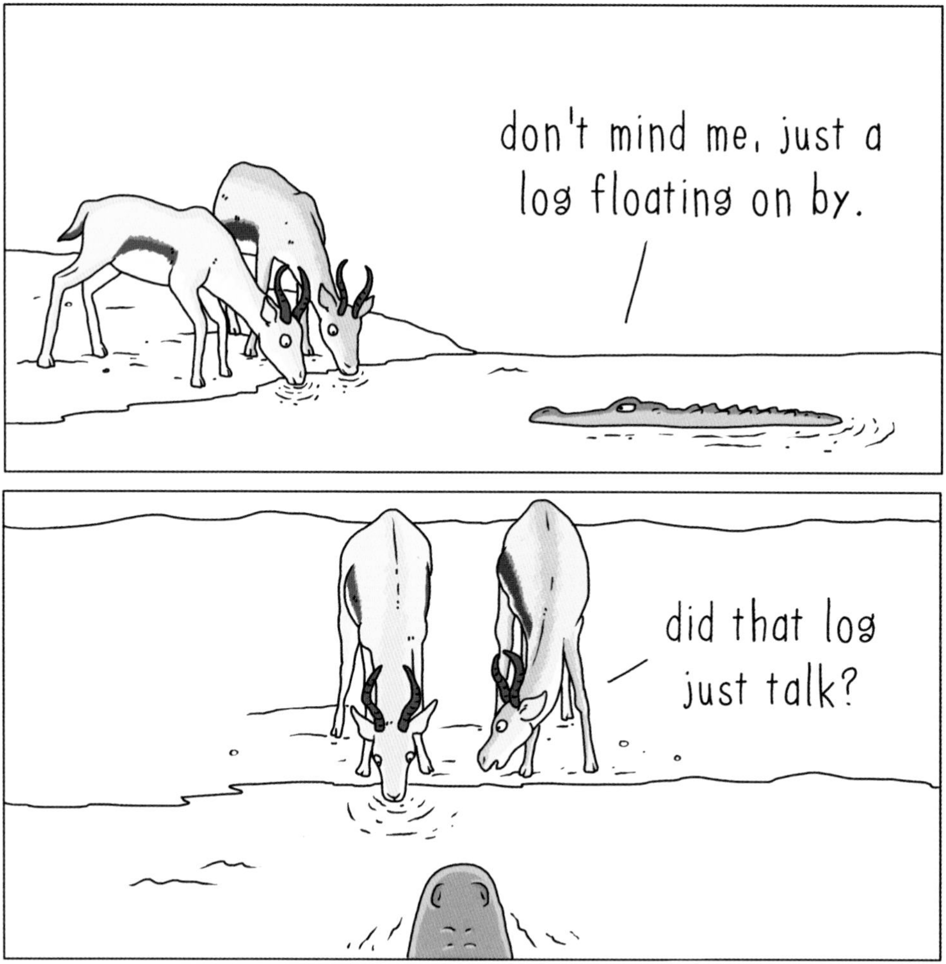
don't mind me, just a log floating on by.
did that log just talk?

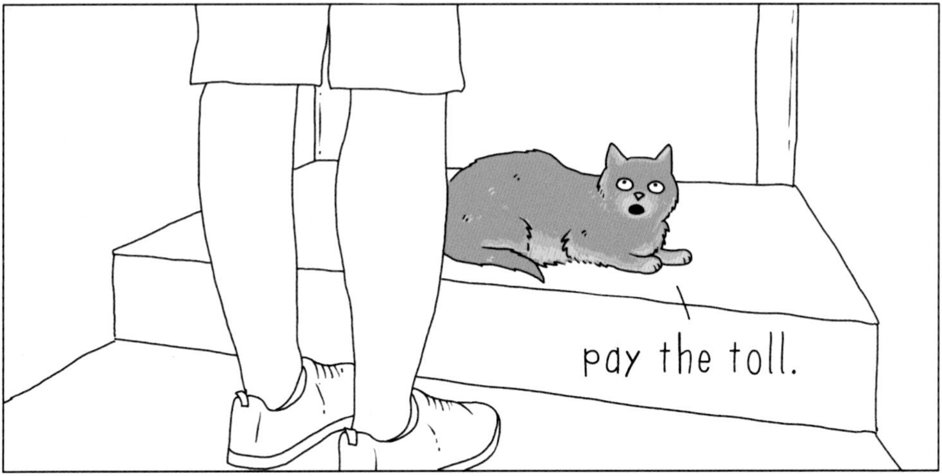
pay the toll.

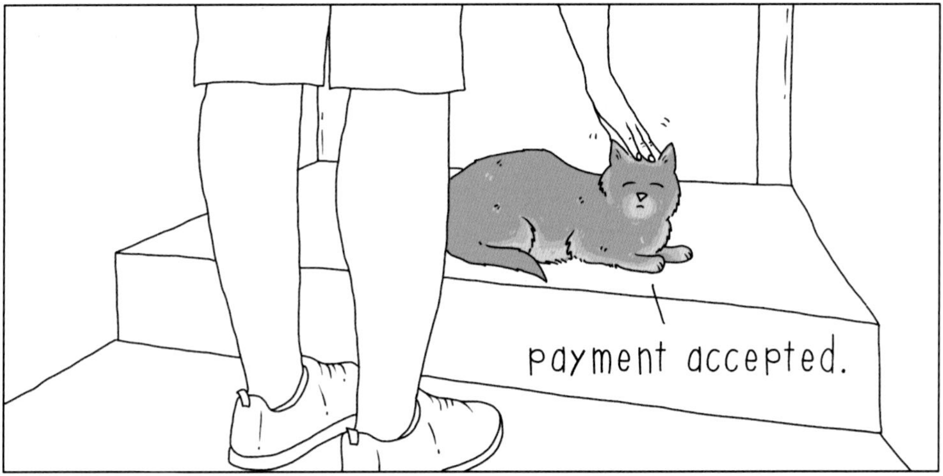
payment accepted.

whoa, someone locked that poor human in a cage and dropped him in the ocean.

don't worry, little buddy.

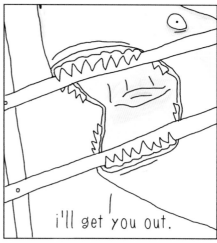

i'll get you out.

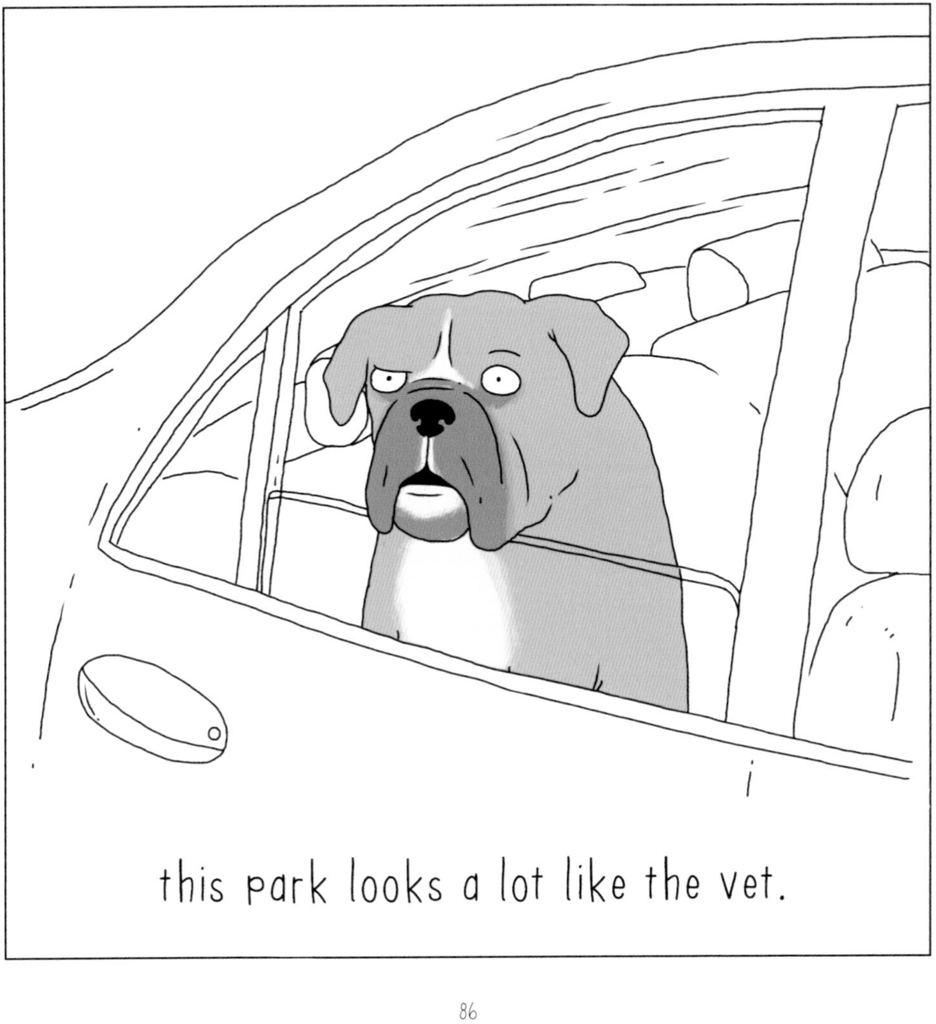

this park looks a lot like the vet.

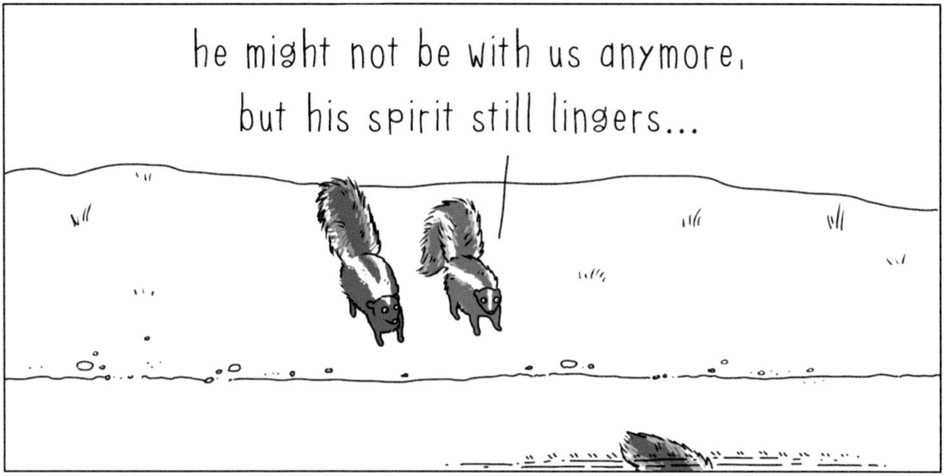
he might not be with us anymore, but his spirit still lingers...

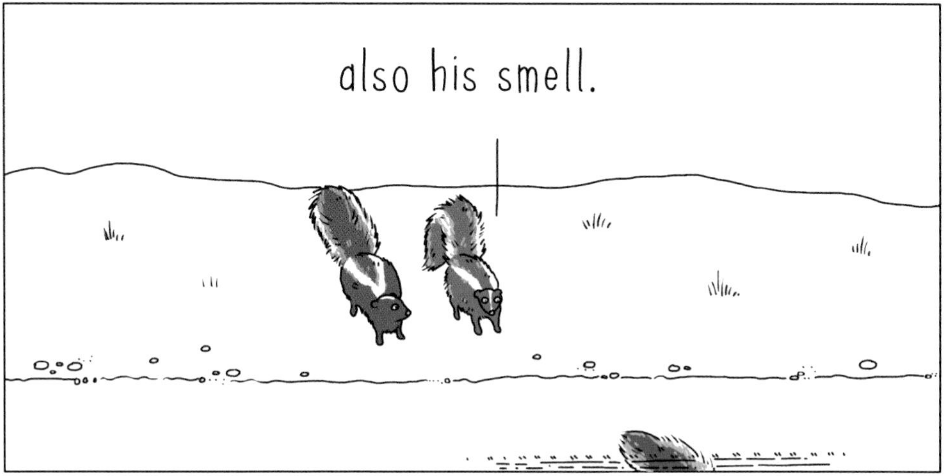
also his smell.

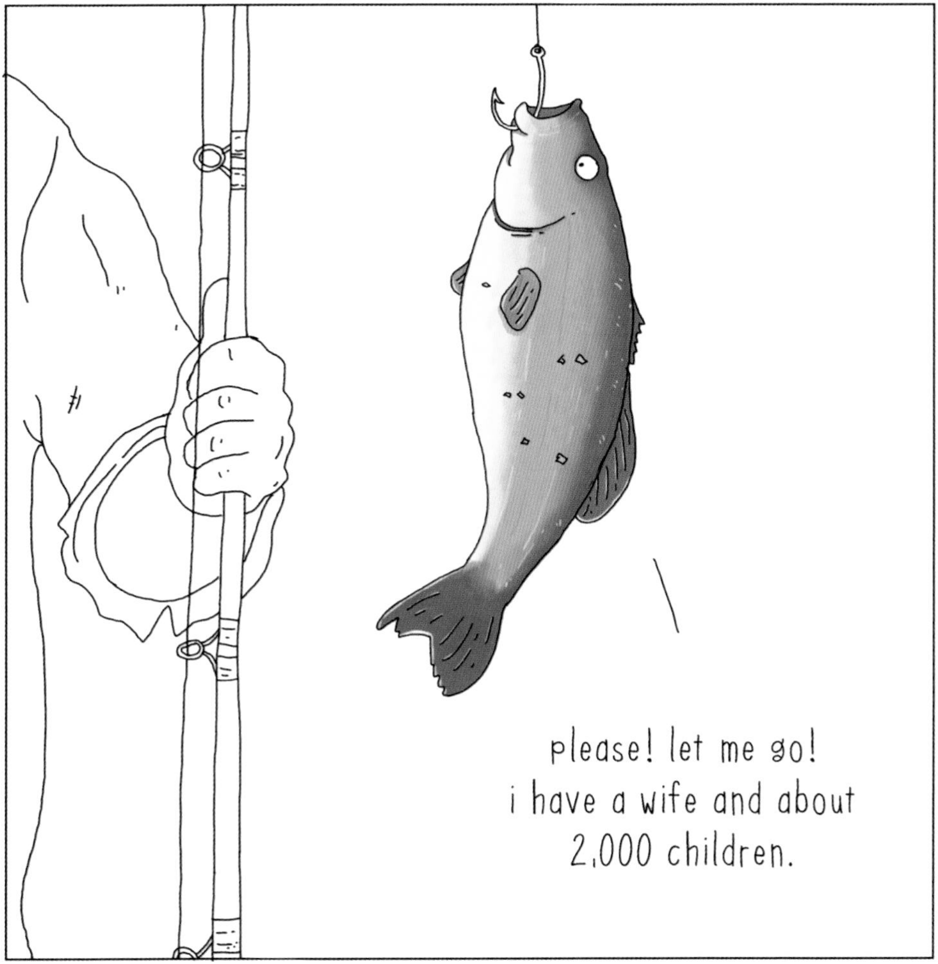
please! let me go!
i have a wife and about
2,000 children.

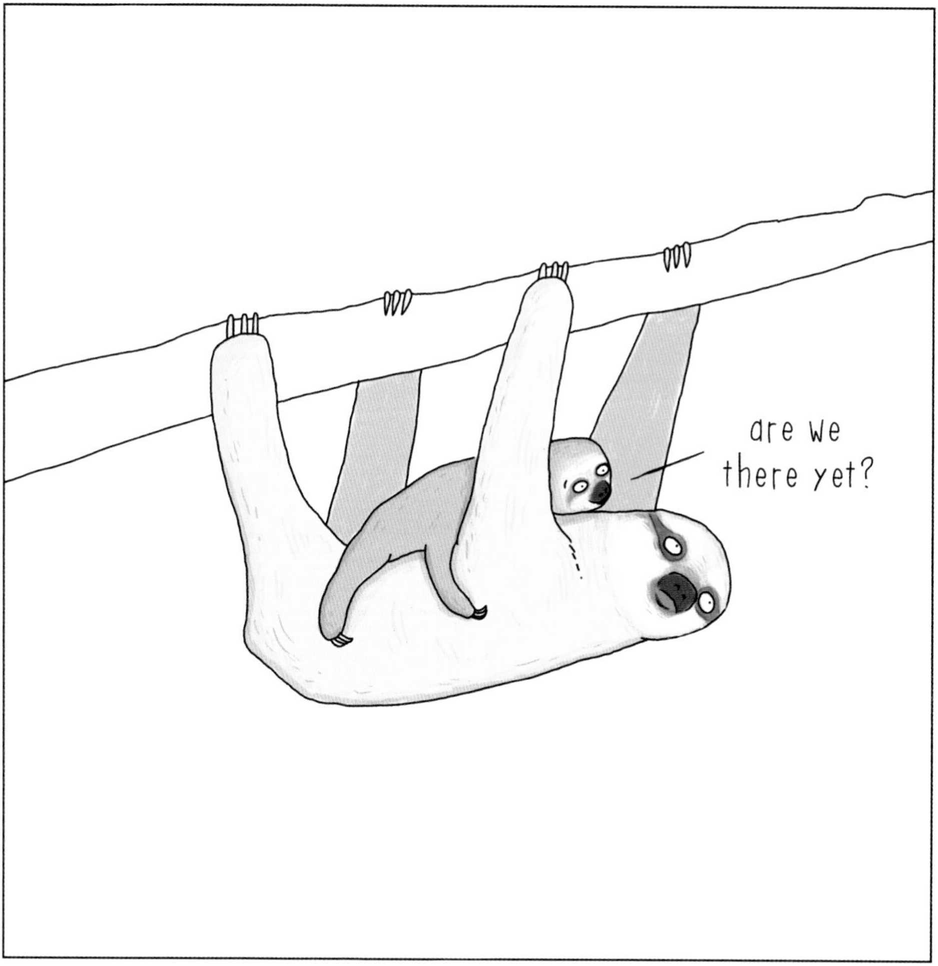
are we
there yet?

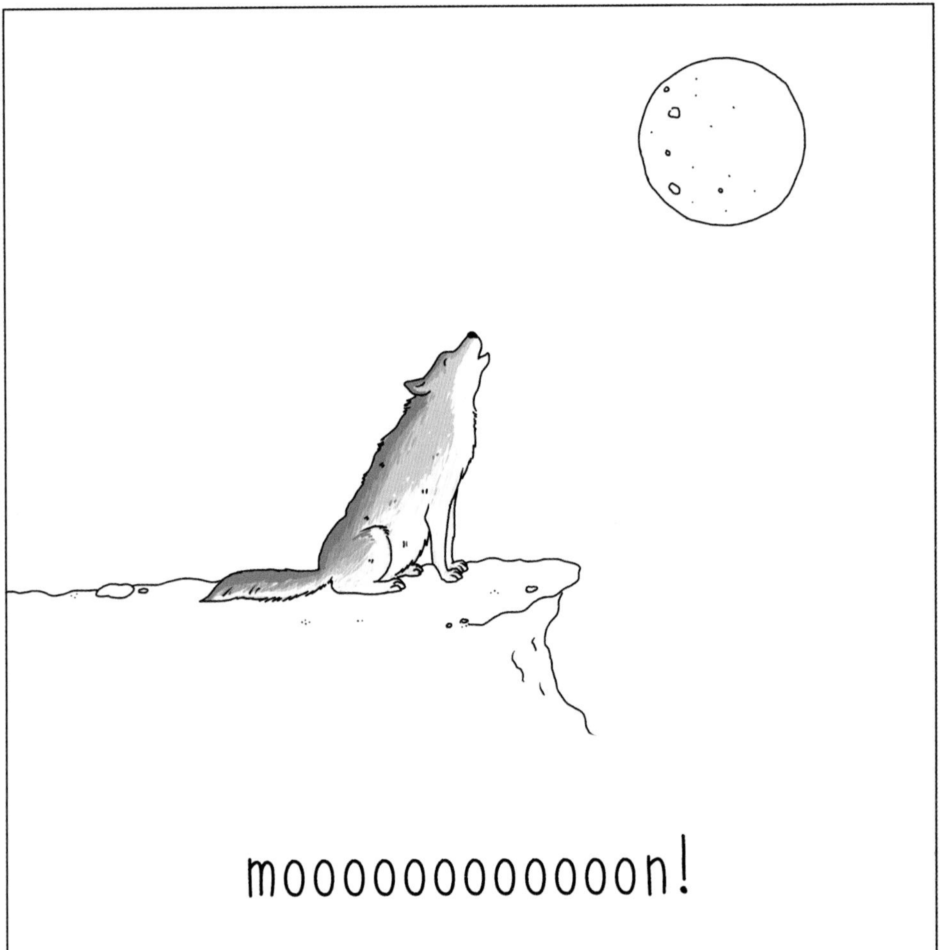
moooooooooooon!

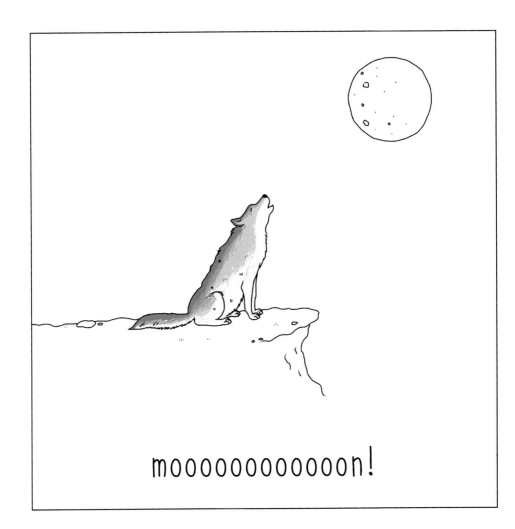

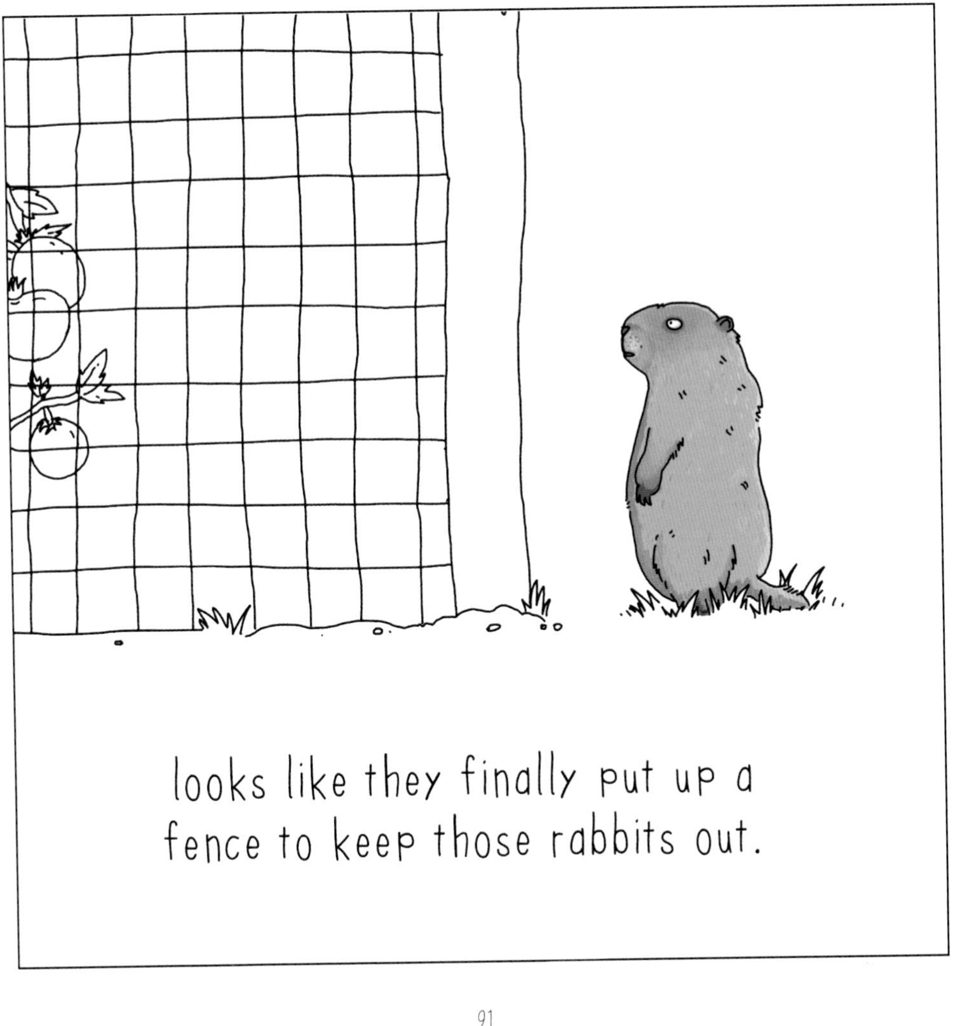

looks like they finally put up a
fence to keep those rabbits out.

wait for it...

wait for it...

GO! GO! GO!

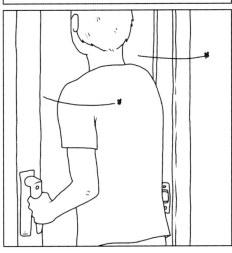

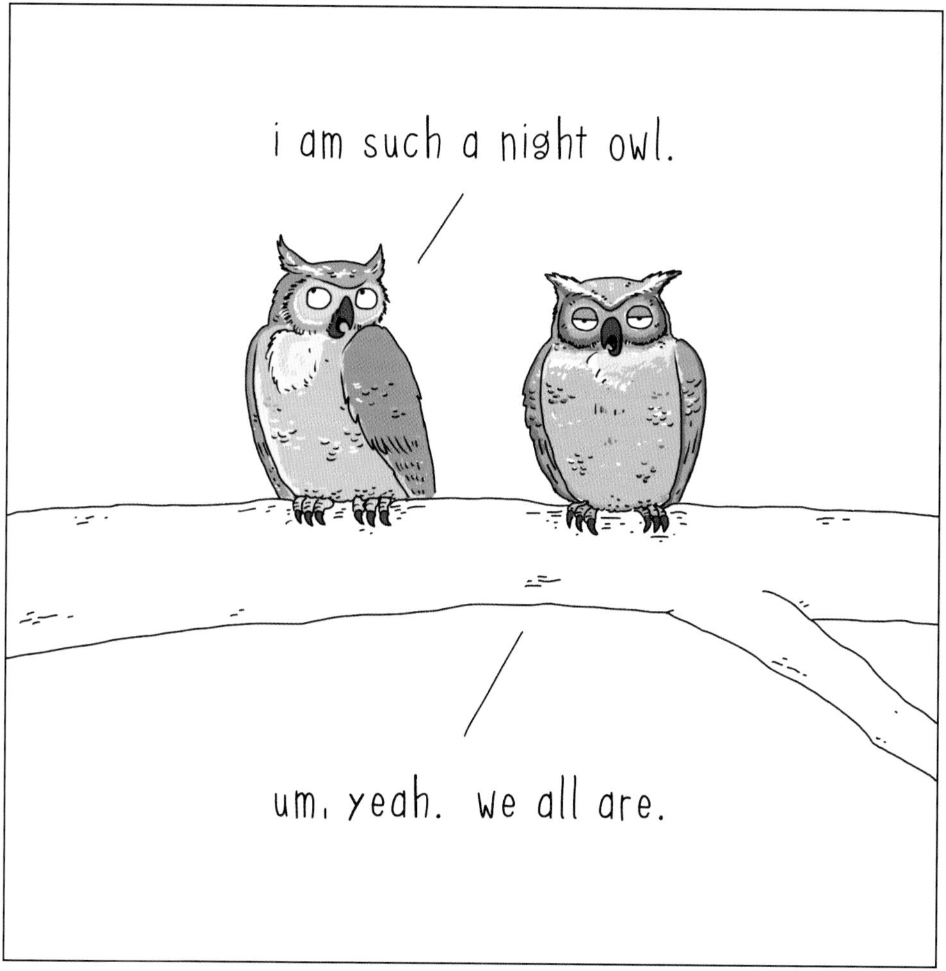
i am such a night owl.
um, yeah. we all are.

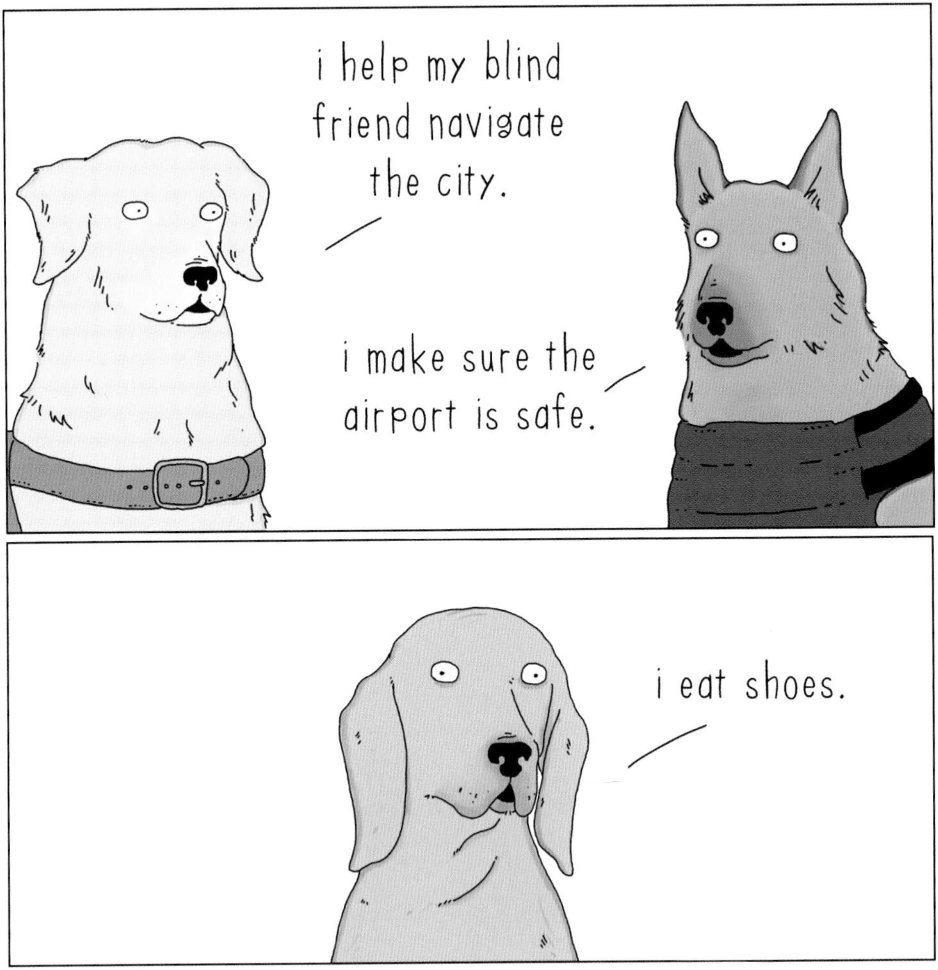
i help my blind friend navigate the city.
i make sure the airport is safe.
i eat shoes.

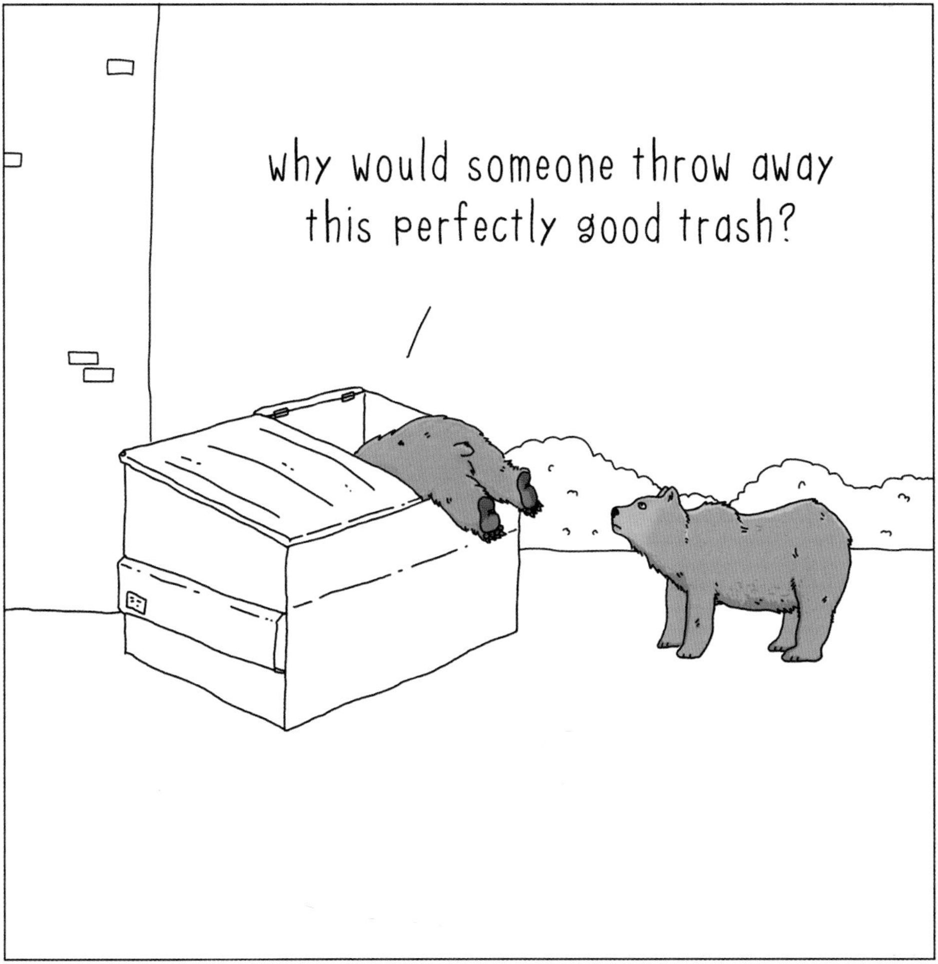
why would someone throw away this perfectly good trash?

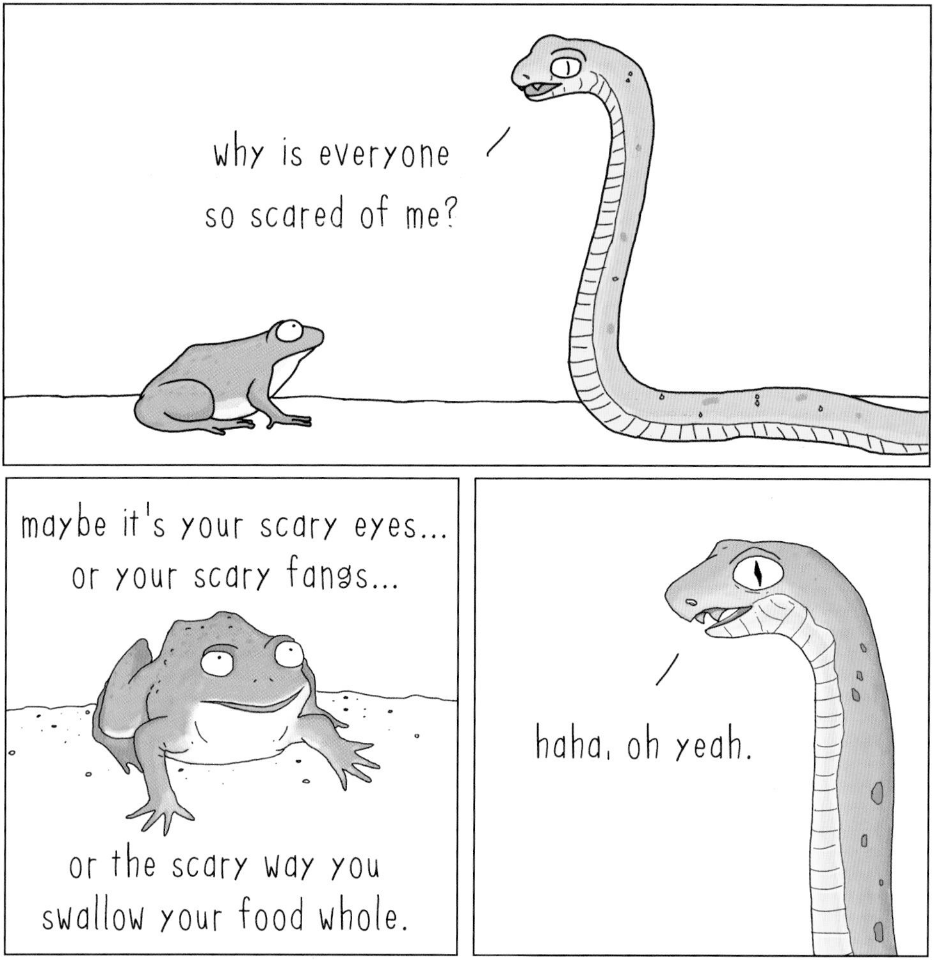
why is everyone so scared of me?
maybe it's your scary eyes...
...or your scary fangs...
or the scary way you swallow your food whole.
haha, oh yeah.

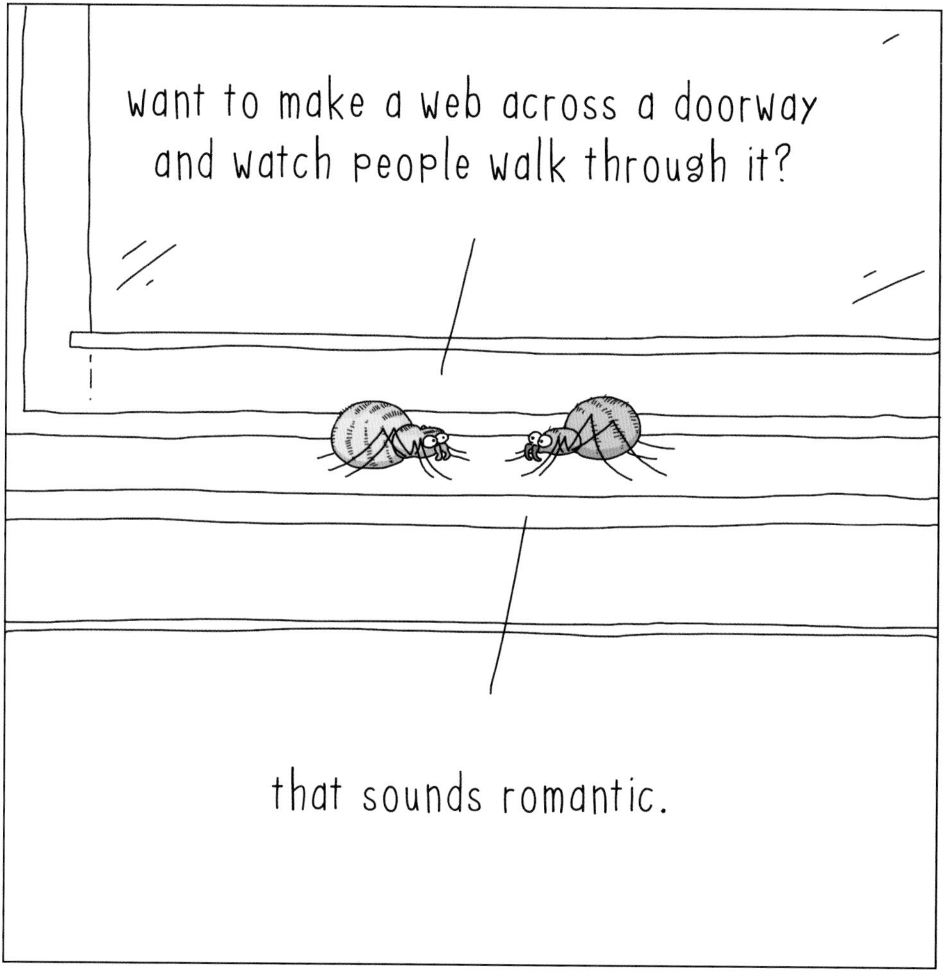
want to make a web across a doorway and watch people walk through it?
that sounds romantic.

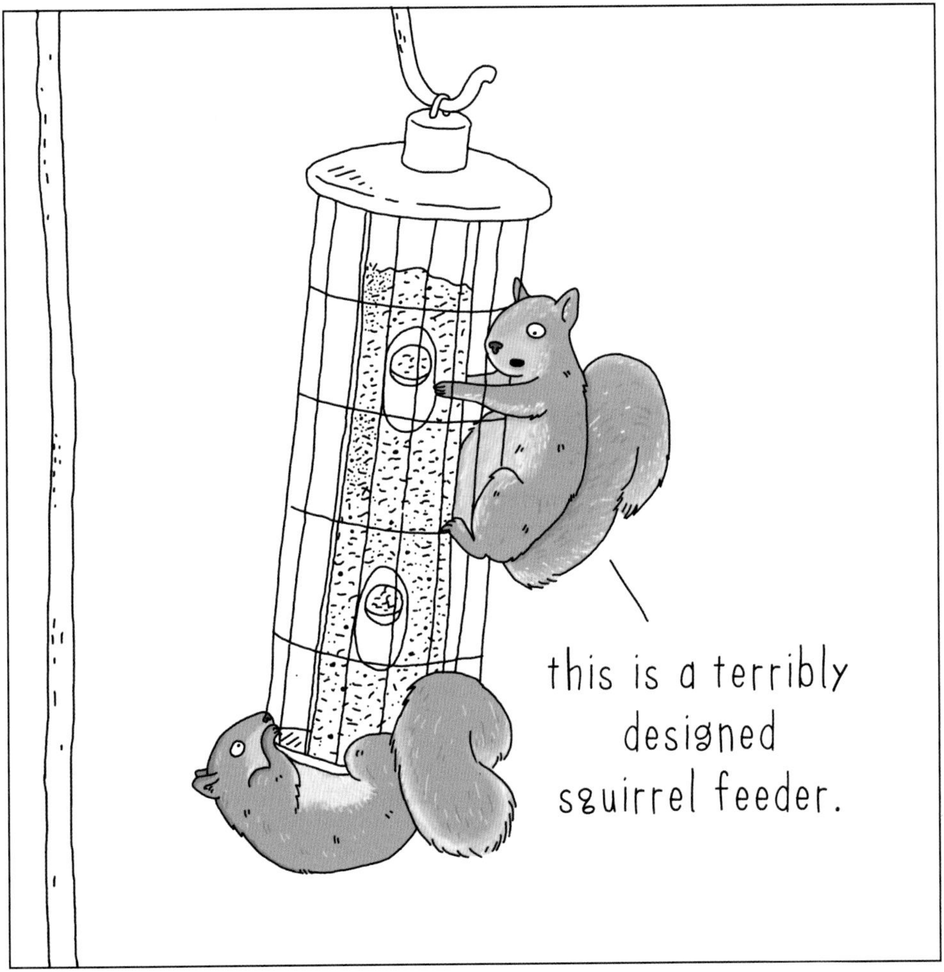
this is a terribly designed squirrel feeder.

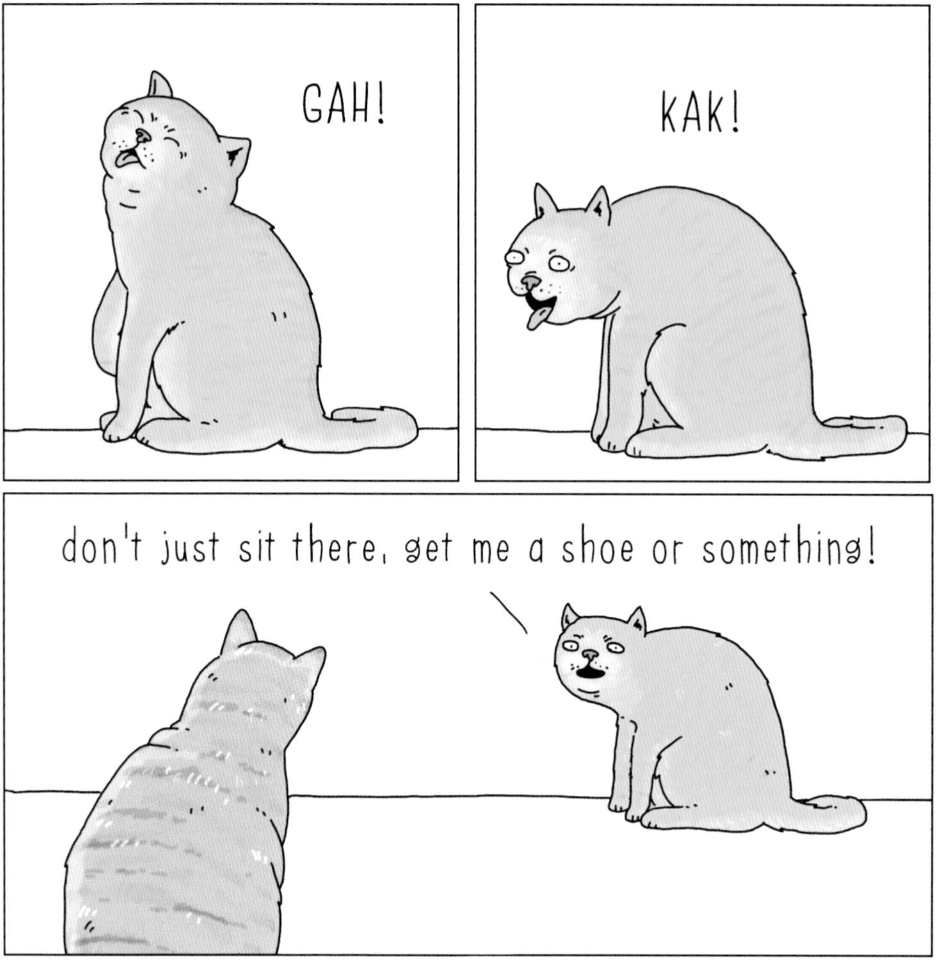
GAH!
KAK!
don't just sit there, get me a shoe or something!

you can't do this every
time i say we need to talk.

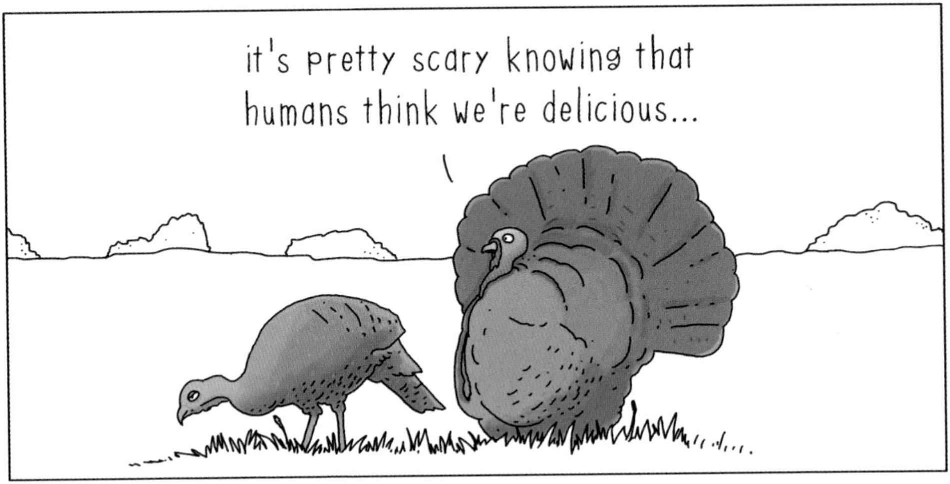
it's pretty scary knowing that humans think we're delicious...

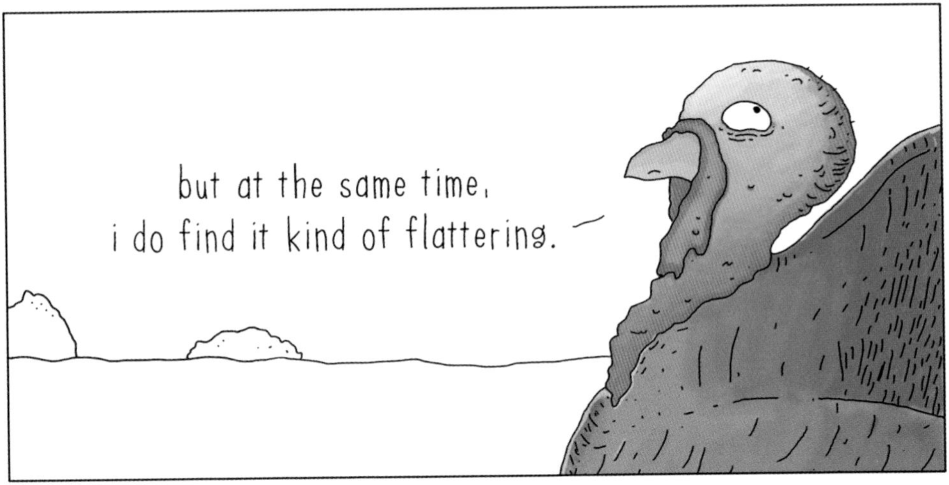
but at the same time, i do find it kind of flattering.

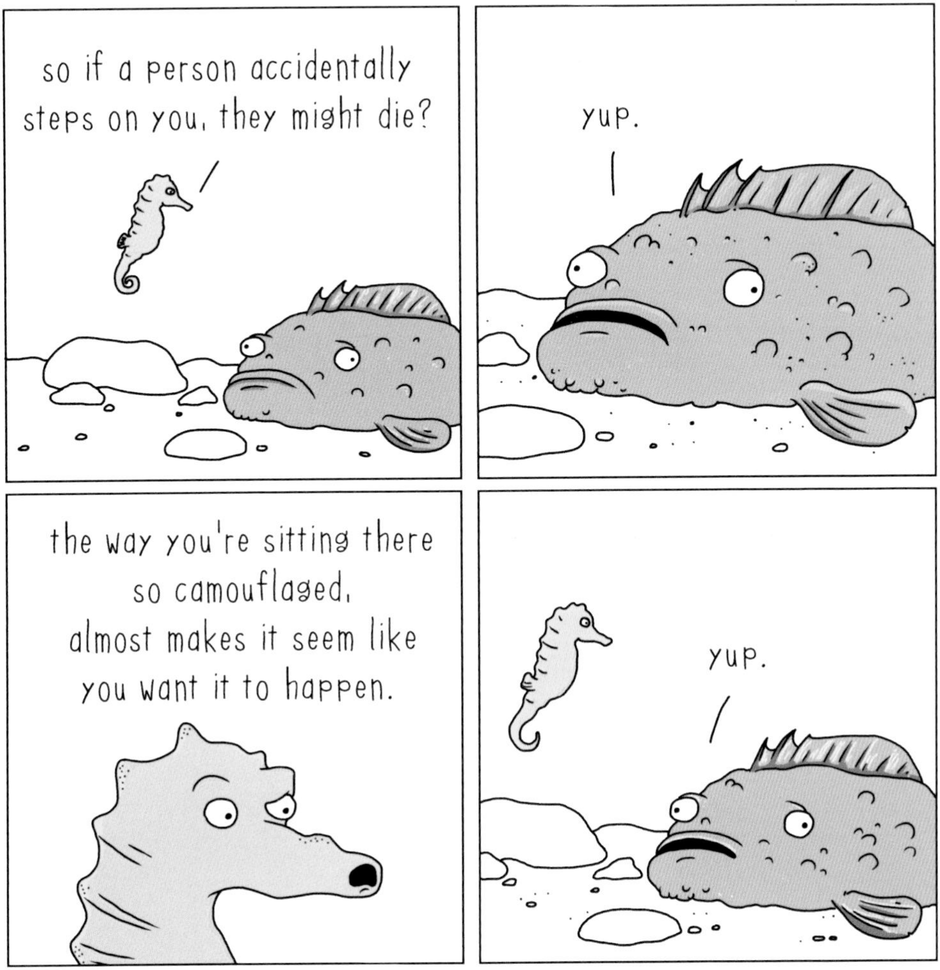
so if a person accidentally steps on you, they might die?
yup.
the way you're sitting there so camouflaged, almost makes it seem like you want it to happen.
yup.

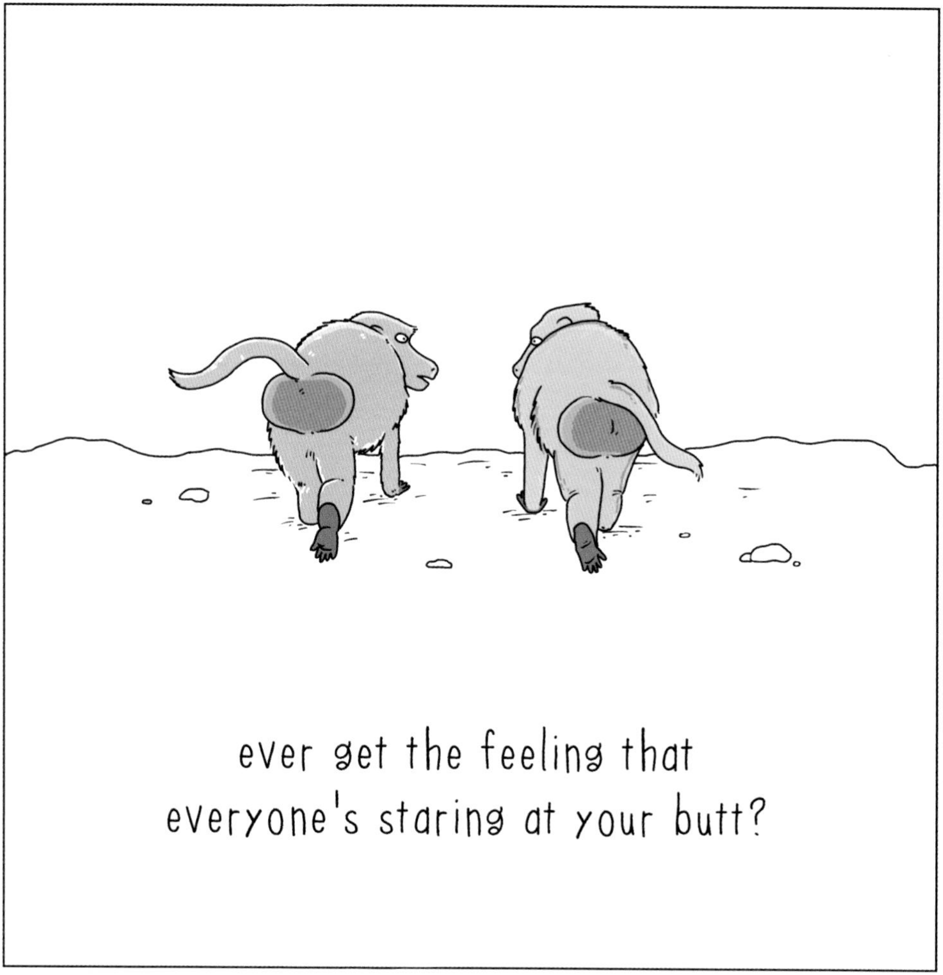
ever get the feeling that
everyone's staring at your butt?

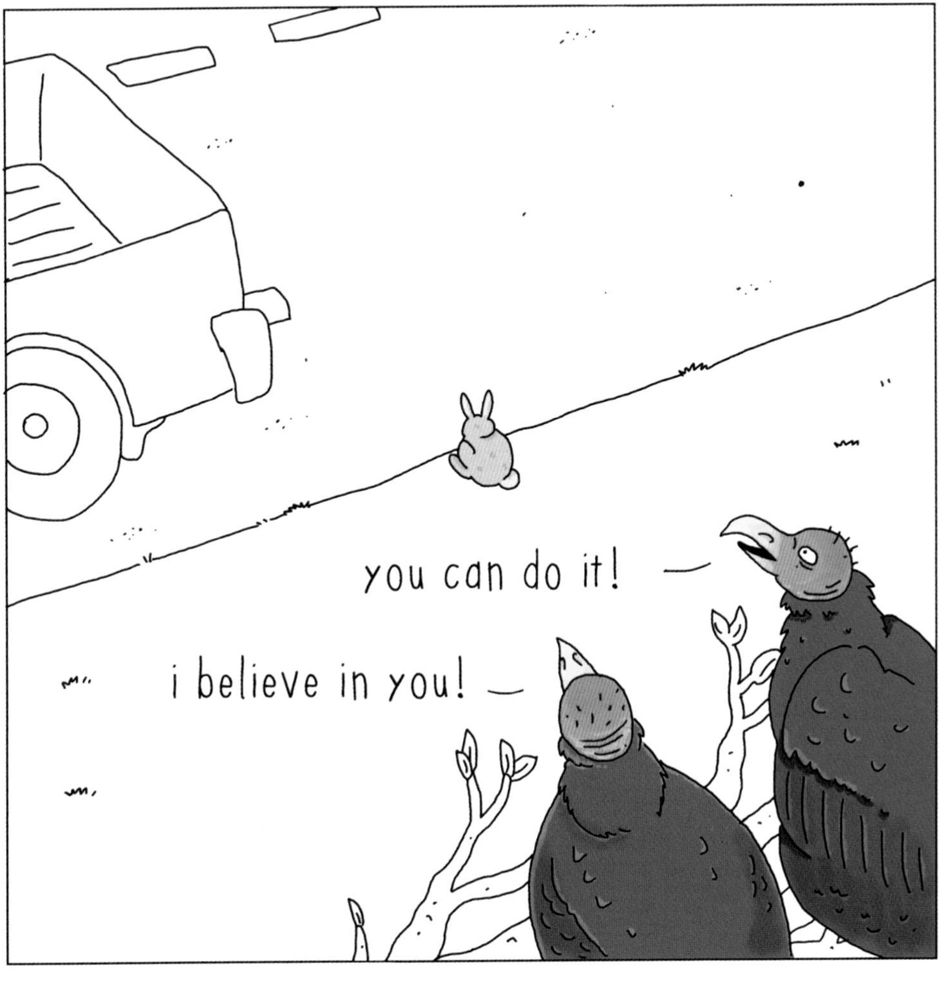
you can do it!
i believe in you!

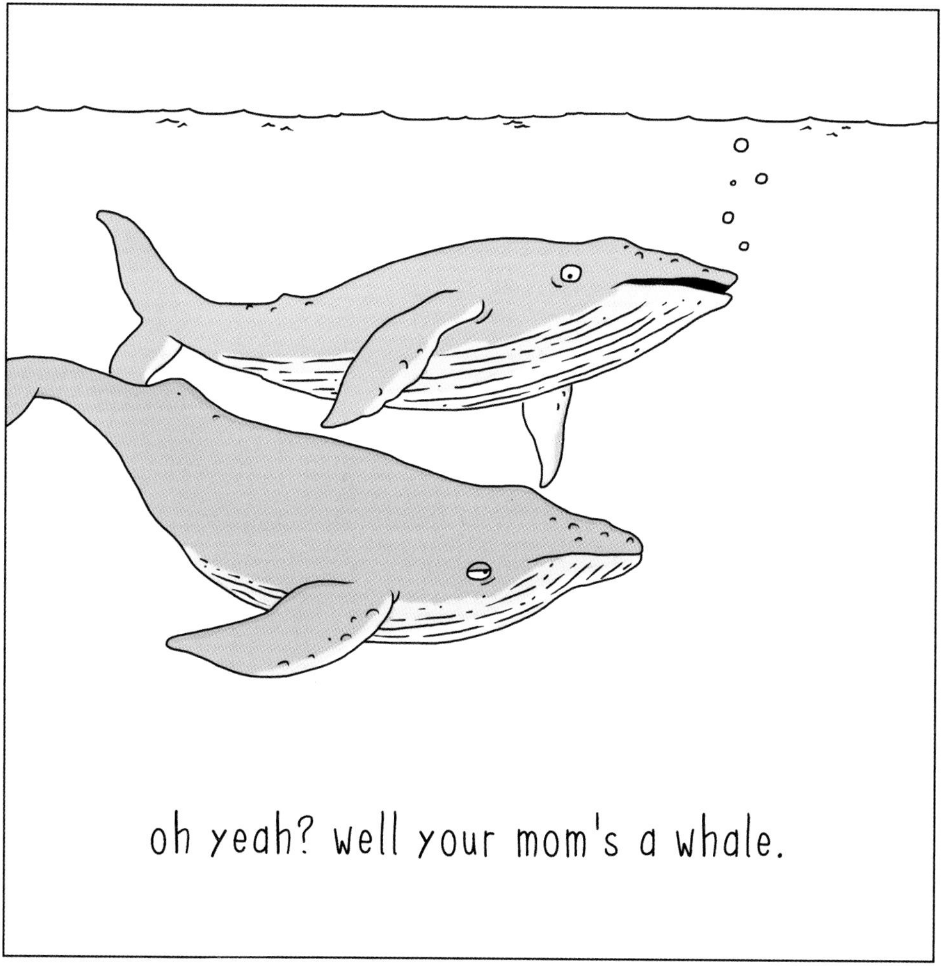
oh yeah? well your mom's a whale.

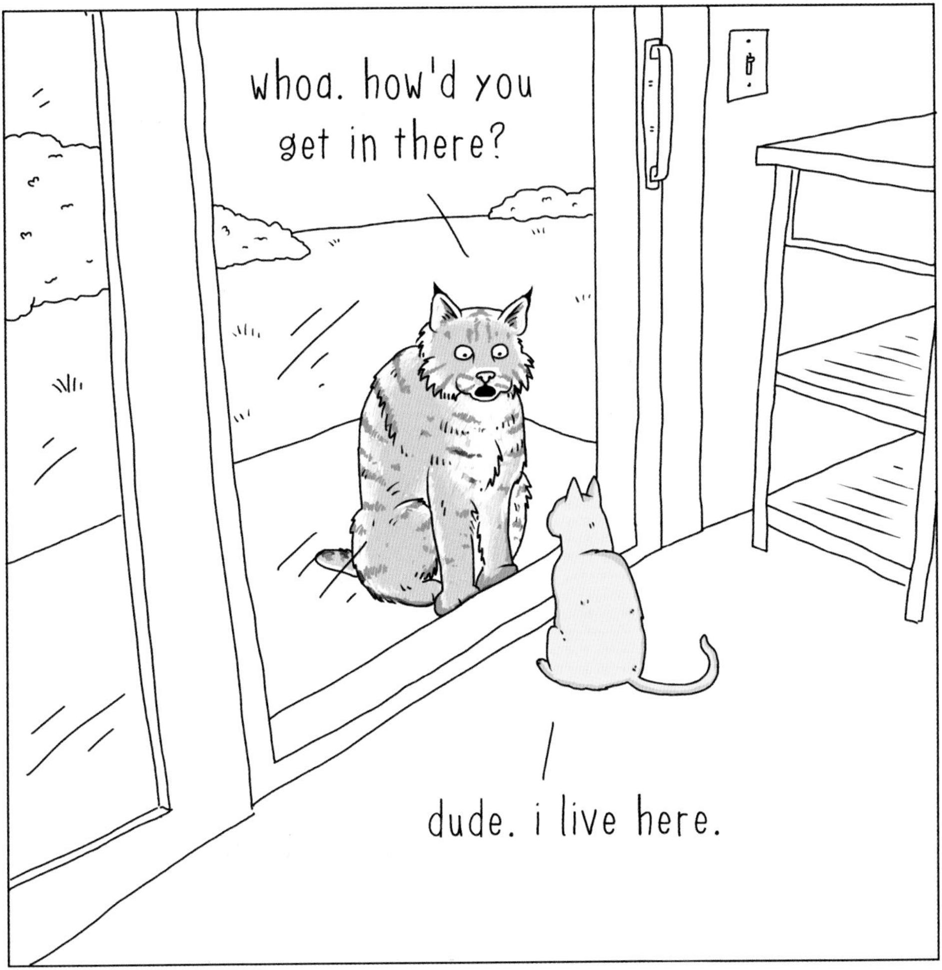
whoa. how'd you get in there?
dude. i live here.

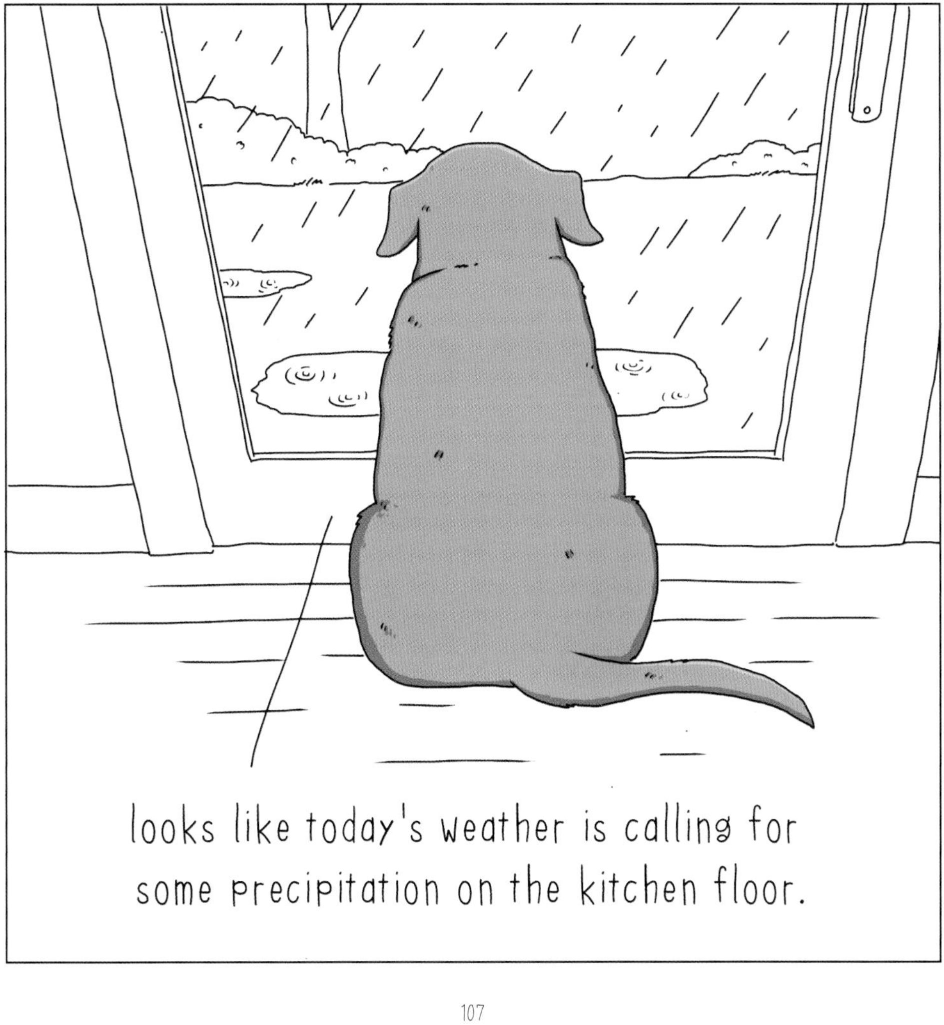

looks like today's weather is calling for
some precipitation on the kitchen floor.

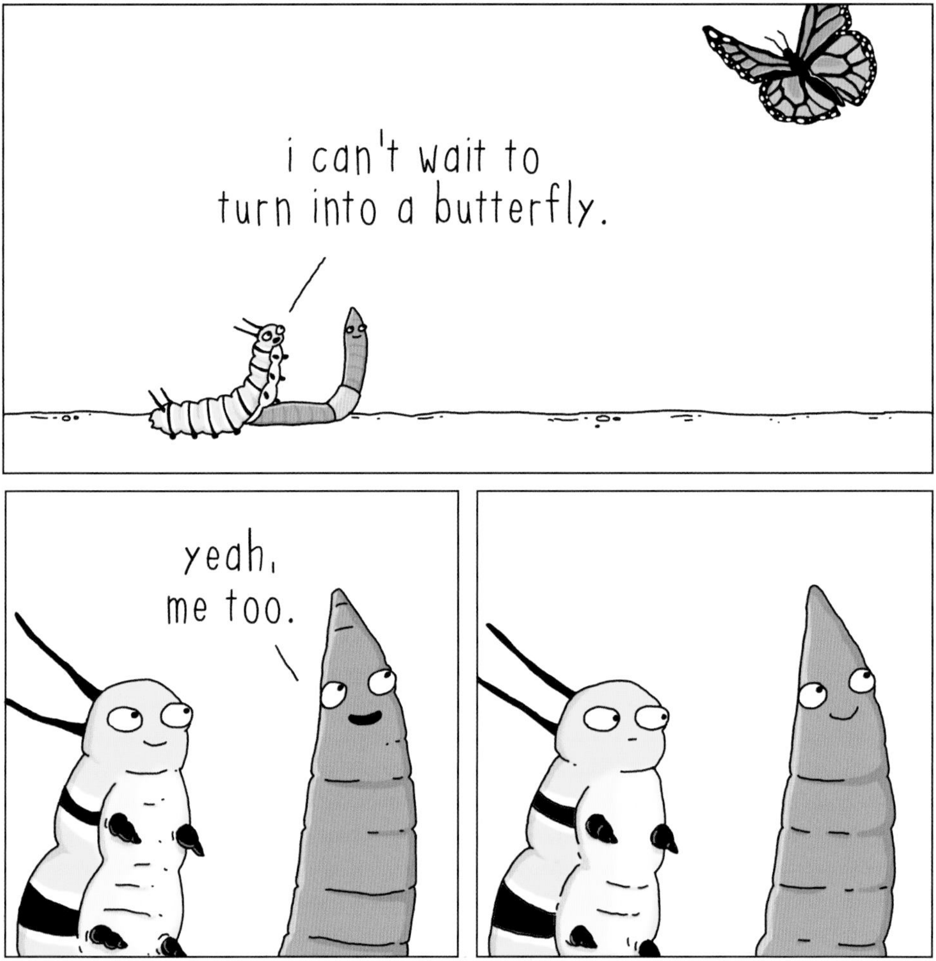
i can't wait to
turn into a butterfly.
yeah,
me too.

about the author

Jimmy Craig is a writer and illustrator based in the Boston area, where he lives with his wife and daughter. His favorite animal is the red panda and he's convinced that if you don't know what a red panda is and take a second to look it up, it'll be your favorite animal soon too. Jimmy is currently working on various projects for Illumination Entertainment.